MILLER'S
Antiques Checklist
CLOCKS

Consultant: John Mighell

General Editors
Judith and Martin Miller

MILLER'S

MILLER'S ANTIQUES CHECKLIST: CLOCKS

Consultant: John Mighell

First published in Great Britain in 1992 by Miller's
an imprint of Reed Consumer Books Limited
Michelin House
81 Fulham Road
London SW3 6RB
and Auckland, Melbourne, Singapore and Toronto

Series Editor	Francis Gertler
Editor	Alfred LeMaitre
Art Editor	Geoff Fennell
Illustrator	Simon Miller
Typesetter	SX Composing Ltd
Production	Sarah Schuman

Reprinted 1994

A CIP catalogue record for this book is available
from the British Library

ISBN 1 85732 945 7

Set in Caslon
Origination by Scantrans Plc., Ltd, Singapore
Produced by Mandarin Offset
Printed in Malaysia

cover picture: *A lacquered bracket clock by James Smith, c.1775* picture on p.1: *An arched brass dial with applied chapter ring and spandrels from a longcase by John Ellicott, c.1710*

A mahogany longcase clock by Robert Jackson, c.1780

CONTENTS

SKELETON CLOCKS

CARRIAGE CLOCKS

MARINE CHRONOMETERS

VIENNA REGULATORS

NOVELTY CLOCKS

HOW TO USE THIS BOOK

When I first started collecting antiques although there were many informative books on the subject I still felt hesitant when it came to actually buying an antique. What I really wanted to do was interrogate the piece – to find out what it was and whether it was genuine.

The *Clocks* Checklist will show you how to assess a piece as an expert would, and provides checklists of questions you should ask before making a purchase. The answer to most (if not all) of the questions should be "yes", but there are always exceptions to the rule: if in doubt, seek expert guidance.

The book is divided into collecting categories, covering both familiar and lesser-known types of clock. At the front of the book is a section covering the parts of a clock, and how the mechanism functions. The book looks at clocks from Britain, Europe and the United States. At the back of the book are a glossary, bibliography and a list of principal makers and marks.

Treat the book as a knowledgeable companion, and soon you will find that antique collecting is a matter of experience, and of knowing how to ask the right questions.

JUDITH MILLER

Each double-page spread looks at a particular category of clock.

The first page shows a carefully chosen representative item of a type that can usually be found at antiques stores or auction houses (rather than only in museums).

The caption gives the date and dimensions of the piece shown, and a code for the price range of this type of article.

A checklist of questions gives you the key to recognizing, dating and authenticating antique pieces of the type shown.

Useful background information is provided about the clockmaker or type of clock.

FRENCH SKELE

A French striking skeleton clock by Balt c.1800; ht 16in/41cm; value code C

Identification checklist for French skeleto
1. Is the frame shaped like an upside-dowr
2. Does the clock have a detachable wood
3. Is the glass dome original?
4. Is there a white enamelled chapter ring
5. Is the bezel engine-turned?
6. Are there any subsidiary dials?

French skeleton clocks
French skeleton clocks are more notable for mechanical refinements than for a flamboyant appearance. They were first produced in the late 18thC, but the majority date from c.1800-70. Most were made by Parisian makers, but never on the same scale as in England. Most are fairly simple in design, with the upside-down letter Y the most common mechanically in the main pi pendulum (see accuracy, a sul date and day o centre seconds French skeleto much less than in the main pi and complex e after today.

128

VALUE CODES
Throughout this book, the caption of the piece in the main picture is followed by a letter which corresponds to the approximate value (at the time of printing) of that piece. The values should be used only as a general guide. The dollar/sterling conversion has been made at a rate of £1=US $1.50; in the event of a change in rate, adjust the dollar value accordingly.

Information helps you to detect fakes, copies and reproductions.

The second page shows you what details to look for.

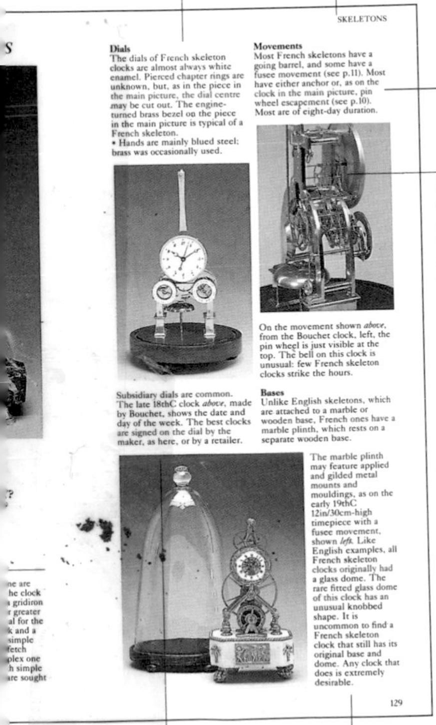

SKELETONS

Dials
The dials of French skeleton clocks are almost always white enamel. Pierced chapter rings are unknown, but, as in the piece in the main picture, the dial centre may be cut out. The engine-turned brass bezel on the piece in the main picture is typical of a French skeleton.
• Hands are mainly blued steel; brass was occasionally used.

Subsidiary dials are common. The late 18thC clock *above*, made by Bouchet, shows the date and day of the week. The best clocks are signed on the dial by the maker, as here, or by a retailer.

Movements
Most French skeletons have a going barrel, and some have a fusee movement (see p.11). Most have either anchor or, as on the clock in the main picture, pin wheel escapement (see p.10). Most are of eight-day duration.

On the movement shown *above*, from the Bouchet clock, left, the pin wheel is just visible at the top. The bell on this clock is unusual: few French skeleton clocks strike the hours.

Bases
Unlike English skeletons, which are attached to a marble or wooden base, French ones have a marble plinth, which rests on a separate wooden base.

The marble plinth may feature applied and gilded metal mounts and mouldings, as on the early 19thC 12in/30cm-high timepiece with a fusee movement, shown *left*. Like English examples, all French skeleton clocks originally had a glass dome. The rare fitted glass dome of this clock has an unusual knobbed shape. It is uncommon to find a French skeleton clock that still has its original base and dome. Any clock that does is extremely desirable.

129

Further photographs and line drawings show:
* items in a different style by the same clockmaker or manufacturer
* unique aspects of the case or of the movement
* similar, but perhaps less valuable clocks that may be mistaken for the more collectable type
* common variations on the piece shown in the main picture
* similar clocks by other makers
* the range of case shapes or decorative features associated with a particular type or period
* fakes and "marriages".

Marks, signatures and serial numbers are explained.

Hints and tips help you to assess factors that affect value – for example, condition and availability.

The codes are as follows:

A £20,000+ ($30,000+)
B £15-20,000 ($22,500-30,000)
C £10-15,000 ($15-22,500)
D £5-10,000 ($7,500-15,000)
E £2-5,000 ($3-7,500)
F £1-2,000 ($1,500-3,000)
G £500-1,000 ($750-1,500)
H under £500 ($750)

INTRODUCTION

Clocks are unique in that they are "living" and working antiques. Some of the more elaborate ones have even been described as "mechanical pictures". A clock also combines – as few other antiques do – the skills of many specialist craftsmen in addition to the clockmaker himself: the skills of the cabinetmaker, polisher, engraver, hand maker, brass caster and dial painter all contribute to the finished product.

Clocks have been an integral part of English domestic furnishing since at least the 17thC, when the lantern clock became the standard domestic timekeeper for the upper and middle classes. From this point, the development of the clock as both timekeeper and decorative object can be traced without a break until the end of the 19thC. The numerous changes in style, size and decoration are readily identifiable, easing the path of the collector through almost 250 years of history. Some clocks, such as the tavern clock or the dial clock, were made to meet a specific social or commercial need. For example, the tavern clock was displayed prominently in coaching inns, where precise timekeeping was a necessity.

Virtually all clocks were signed by the maker on the dial and/or the movement. Because of the tight control exercised by the Clockmakers Company – the governing body of the profession, founded in 1631 – records of practically all makers have survived. Although these are often brief, we have at least some information about most of the important English clockmakers. By contrast, the cabinetmaker seems never to have signed the case, so almost nothing is known about this aspect of the trade. As will be seen from the bibliography, the history of clocks and their makers has been extensively researched. Not only are there now many works on various styles and periods, but also numerous in-depth studies of regional, or provincial clockmaking, and even of individual makers. The collector can thus arm himself with a wealth of background information before making a purchase. In fact, it is an extremely useful first step to purchase a reference book covering the intended area of collecting, together with one of the standard reference works on the history of clocks and clockmaking. With the knowledge that these will provide, expensive mistakes can be avoided.

The typical collector is likely to want to acquire examples of several types of clock, such as longcase, wall, bracket or carriage, to suit the style or period of his or her house or furniture. Those who choose to specialize can quite easily assemble a modest collection in such areas as carriage clocks, English dial clocks or four-glass bracket clocks. Some collectors may seek the work of an individual maker. Carriage clocks, in particular, were produced in very large numbers by even the most important makers, and there are an extraordinary number of sizes and shapes for the collector to choose from. Others may choose to concentrate on makers within a single English county, region or town. Provincial makers, particularly those distant from London, frequently developed individual and clearly identifiable styles. Clocks by American and Continental makers come in a host of styles, often with unique mechanical features, and their value ranges widely.

As with any antique, condition is critical in the decision whether or not to buy, and to the price to be paid. Because a clock may be a very complex mechanism, condition and originality must be carefully assessed by the potential purchaser. There are pitfalls; the classic example is a longcase movement and dial which are out of period or do not fit the case. Dials and hands may have been replaced, and the case may have undergone excessive restoration. Even worse, from time to time longcase and bracket clocks appear in cases which have been constructed in recent years. Many of these are skilful reproductions, which can fool all but the experienced eye. With carriage clocks, the working mechanism, or movement, may be a modern replacement, simply because a clockmaker did not have the skills necessary to overhaul the original. However, in a relatively short time, the beginner can acquire at least the basic knowledge required to make a sound technical assessment of a particular clock. Above all, it is important to develop an eye for line and for proportion. Whatever, the mechanical refinements of a particular clock, visual appeal and the right proportion will always be of key importance in making the decision to purchase.

Background reading can help, but there is really no substitute for the experience gained by looking at and handling as many clocks as possible. This is where knowledgeable and patient dealers can really prove their worth. Visits to auction rooms also provide an ideal opportunity to study clockmaking in all its forms, from the very finest pieces to the most ordinary and workaday. Where possible, any museum with a significant clock collection should also be visited.

It is fashionable to talk of value when discussing antiques, and clocks are no exception. However, it is important to remember that virtually no two clocks are identical in every respect. There may be subtle differences of figuring in wood veneers, of patina and of proportion on which no precise value can be set. One dealer with a lifetime's experience may value a particular clock more highly than another with only a general knowledge of the subject. Whatever the price, the clock on which you finally set your heart will ultimately give the greatest satisfaction. Prices can go down as well as up, but a good quality clock will always prove to be a good investment. Above all, only buy a particular clock if you like the look of it and are convinced you will be happy with it.

JOHN MIGHELL

CLOCKS

There are certain basic features common to all antique clocks, an understanding of which is useful in assessing the age (and the authenticity) of any piece.

The parts of a clock

The key elements of any clock consist of:

* the mechanism, or *movement.*
* the *case* (houses the clock)
* the *dial* (shows the time)

MOVEMENTS

The movement consists of a system of brass and steel wheels and gears, known as the *train*. It is usually housed between two brass plates; some clocks have wooden plates and movements.

The escapement

The escape wheel, or *escapement*, controls the speed at which a clock runs, thereby regulating its timekeeping. It releases, at equal intervals, the energy from hanging weights or a coiled spring, and transmits it from the movement to the hands. The escapement is usually an arm with two *pallets*, which engage with the teeth of the escape wheel. The main types include:

* the *balance wheel escapement*, used until c.1670. The earliest form of balance, the *foliot*, is found on some of the earliest English lantern clocks.
* the *verge escapement*
* the *anchor escapement.*

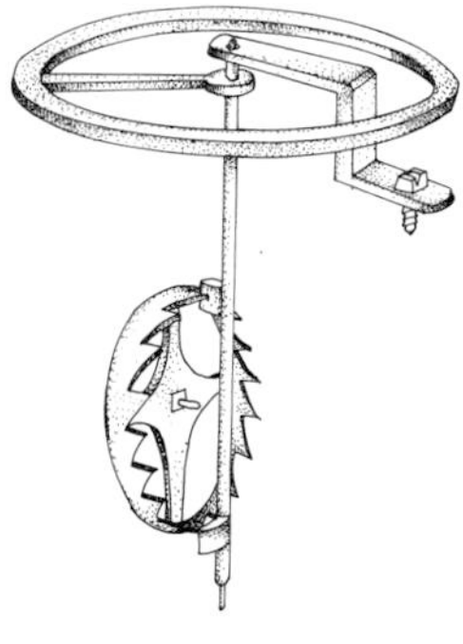

* The oscillating *balance wheel*, *above*, releases in turn the two pallets, or "flags", on the vertical bar, which engage the toothed wheel. The balance was difficult to regulate.

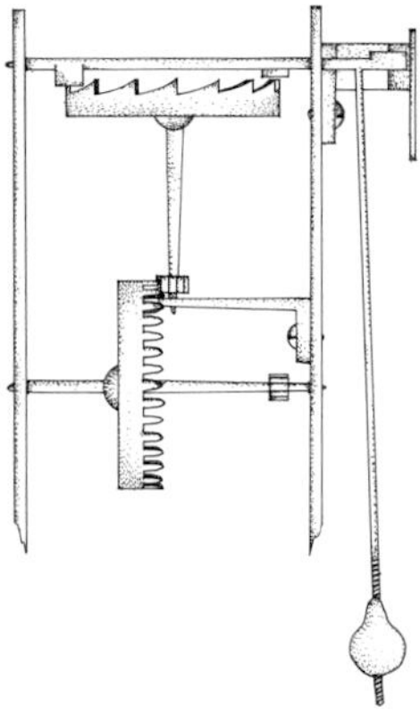

* The *verge escapement*, *above*, also uses pallets, but the short pendulum enabled the clock to be more accurately regulated. The verge was used on lantern clocks, as well as on most bracket clocks. The bulbous *pendulum bob* is typical of early verge escapements; later ones are flat. By adjusting the position of the bob, the pendulum swings faster or slower.

* The *anchor escapement*, *above*, was used – first in longcases – from c.1670, and became standard for longcases, brackets, and many wall clocks. The anchor engages at intervals with the teeth of the escape wheel. The pallets may push these slightly backwards; this is known as *recoil*.
* Clocks with an anchor may have a long or short pendulum.
* Many bracket clocks have been converted to an anchor. The anchor pendulum swings in a smaller arc than that on a verge, and has a disc-shaped bob.

Other escapements
* Many carriage clocks have a *lever* (or *platform lever*) escapement, with no pendulum.
* The cylinder escapement is found on inexpensive late 19thC French carriage clocks.
* The chronometer escapement is found mainly in chronometers.
* The pin wheel is a form of anchor used by French makers.

The pendulum
Most weight-driven clocks (and most spring-driven ones), have a *pendulum* to control the clock's speed. The pendulum was used from the mid-17thC, and made clocks much more accurate.
* A pendulum swings in a regular arc. It is connected to the same *arbor* (shaft) on which the escape wheel turns.
* The pendulum is a brass or steel rod, with a metal disc, or *bob*, at the bottom (usually lead cased in brass). The bob's position alters timekeeping.
* On a verge escapement, the bob is usually on a threaded rod.
* On an anchor escapement, the bob slides on the rod and can be adjusted by a *rating nut*.

Pendulum variations
The length of the rod varies with temperature, affecting timekeeping. The longer the rod, the greater its swing, and so the slower the clock. To avoid variations, compensating pendulums were developed.

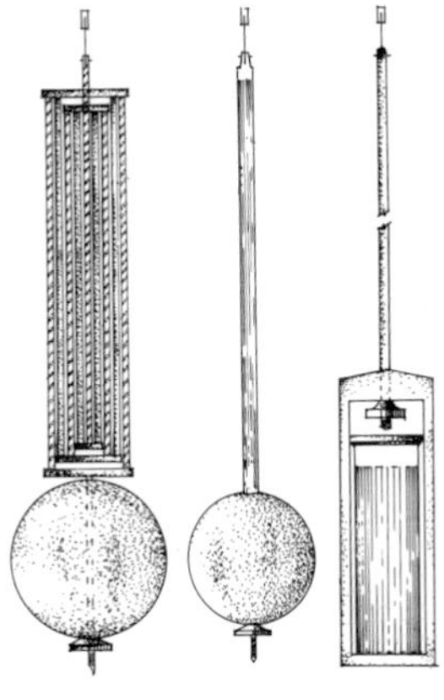

Variations include:
* *gridiron*, *left*; up to nine zinc and steel rods, which expand and contract at differing rates, compensating for changes in length.
* *wood rod*, *below centre*; wood is little affected by cold or heat.
* *mercury jar*, *below right*; the expansion of the mercury in the jar counters that of the rod.
* Some bracket clocks have a *rise and fall dial* to adjust swing.

Power
Clocks are powered in two ways:
* *weight-driven*; by the pull of hanging weights (lantern, longcase and some wall clocks)
* *spring-driven*; by the release of energy in a coiled spring (bracket, carriage, skeleton, novelty and some wall clocks).

Weights
Weights are brass-cased lead, or plain lead or iron. They should always match or at least look the same age, if replaced.
* Weights are hung on a line. It must be replaced periodically.

Controlling the spring
On spring-driven clocks, the spring loses force as the clock runs. Most English spring-driven clocks – notably brackets – have a device known as a *fusee*, to spread power over the running time of the clock.

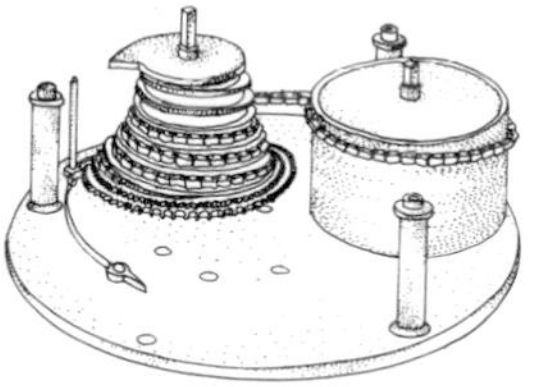

The *fusee*, *above*, is a conical spool, which takes up a chain, wire or gut line wound around the spring barrel. As the spring unwinds, it turns the barrel, pulling the fusee line round it. The line unwinds first from the narrow end, when the power of the spring is greatest. By the end of the duration (usually eight days), the line is taken from the wide end, making up for the weakness of the spring.
* Striking clocks have two trains, with a fusee for each.
* On most French and many other Continental clocks, there is no fusee. Instead, these have a *going barrel*: power is transmitted directly from the spring to the train. The fusee allows more accurate timekeeping.

Duration
The length of time a clock runs before needing winding is its *duration*. In weight-driven clocks, the duration is the time the weight takes to fall; in spring-driven clocks, how long the spring takes to unwind. Most longcases are of eight-day duration.
* Most clocks are wound with a crank or key through one or more holes in the dial, known as *winding holes*.

The striking mechanism
Many clocks can strike the hours. These clocks have two separate *trains* (sets of wheels). The simplest examples strike the hours only.
* On some clocks, a *strike/silent dial*, marked "strike" and "silent", turns off the striking without affecting the running of the clock.

Types of striking
There are two ways to control the number of hours struck:
* the *countwheel*, or *locking plate*: a slotted wheel on the backplate.
* the *rack* (or "*rack and snail*"): a more reliable mechanism, matching the striking with the movements of the hands. It was used from c.1675.

The bell
Until c.1840, the hours were struck on a bell (a few strike on a wire gong), made from a mixture of alloys known as "bell metal".
* From c.1840, the gong became standard. Some early carriage clocks (c.1830-70) have a bell.

Complicated striking
Some clocks strike the half- or quarter-hours as well as the hours. They have a third train, a third weight (or spring), and three winding holes. The main types are:
* *grande sonnerie*; repeats the last hour after each quarter-hour
* *petite sonnerie*; strikes the hours and quarter-hours only.
* the *repeat mechanism*; appears as a pull-cord or a button on the case. If the cord is pulled or the button pressed, the clock repeats the last hour or quarter-hour. The best clocks repeat both.
* Clocks with complicated striking are more valuable than those with simple hour-striking.
* Cleaning and repair of complex striking requires expert attention.

Maintenance
Clocks can suffer wear due to lack of maintenance. Movements need overhauling every seven to ten years.

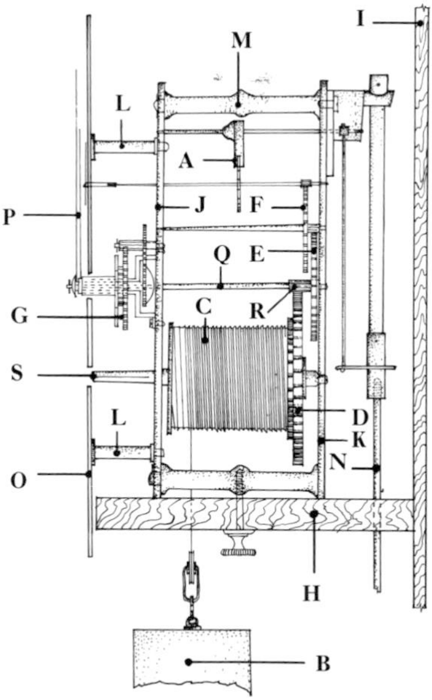

PARTS OF A CLOCK
The main components of a simple weight-driven clock, as shown *left*, include:
A anchor escapement
B weight
C barrel
D main wheel
E centre wheel
F third wheel
G dial wheels
H seatboard
I backboard
J front plate
K backplate
L dial feet
M pillars
N pendulum
O dial plate
P hands
Q centre arbor
R pinions
S winding arbor

THE DIAL

The *dial* shows the time, and is the "face" of the clock. It consists of a square, arched or round metal (or wooden) plate, known as the *dial plate*. A ring, called the chapter ring, shows the hour and minute divisions. Except for carriage clocks, most clocks are wound from the front.

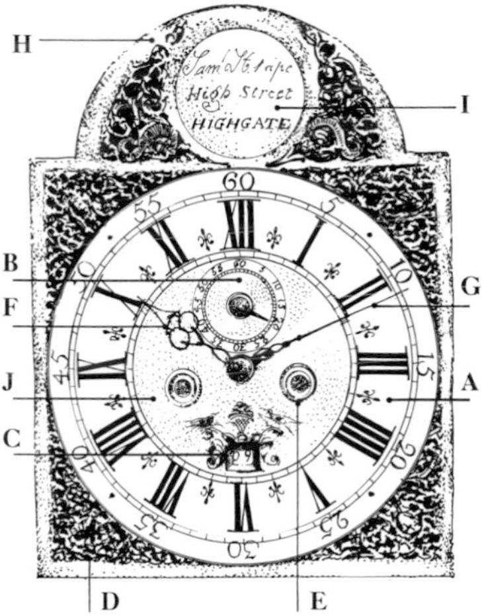

PARTS OF THE DIAL

The basic parts of the dial, as on the 18thC arched example, shown *left*, include:

A chapter ring
B subsidiary dial
C calendar aperture
D applied corner spandrels (usually brass)
E winding holes
F hour hand
G minute hand
H dial arch
I engraved boss (may also be a strike/silent lever)
J "matted" centre

Types of dial

Dials can be dated by shape:

* *square*; used from the early 17th to the early 18thC; popular with English provincial makers until the 1840s (usually in painted metal rather than brass).
* *arched*; introduced c.1715, and standard on London-made longcase and bracket clocks from 1720-25.
* *round*; used especially in France, and very common in the 19thC.

Dial materials also provide a clue to dating a clock:

* *Brass*, with applied chapter ring. This was the earliest type of dial, used on lantern clocks and most early longcases. From c.1780, one-piece brass is more common.
* *Painted wood*; common on 18thC Continental clocks, as well as on English wall clocks, and on some American clocks.
* *Painted metal*; very common during the 19thC.
* *Enamelled metal*; also known as porcelain; used on most French clocks and most carriage clocks.

Brass dials

From the 17thC, dials were made from brass sheet, with a "matted" (hammered) centre. The chapter ring was fixed by means of small feet. Cast brass *spandrels* were applied to the corners; some early 17thC clocks have engraved corners.

* One-piece silvered brass dials, with an integral chapter ring, were less costly to make.
* Brass dials are attached to the movement by brass rods known as *feet*. These are riveted to the dial plate and fit into holes in the frontplate. Feet should always fit their original holes.

Silvered brass dials

Silvered dials are finished with a silvering compound. If worn or rubbed off, the plain brass finish will be visible. Re-silvering is acceptable. The engraved numerals and signature are filled with black wax (to which the silvering does not adhere). The wax is durable, and seldom needs to be replaced. If it has dried out, it is easy to replace.

Wooden dials

Early English wooden dials are painted black, with gilt numerals. Later wooden dials have a white ground and black numerals. Most Black Forest clocks have wooden dials. Tiny cracks caused by the expansion and contraction of the wood are indicative of authenticity. If cracks are only on the back, the dial has been restored.

Painted metal dials
Painted metal dials are usually iron, with figures and signature painted in black on a white ground. They were popular because they were inexpensive, easy to read and featured colourful decoration.
* A network of fine cracking, or *crazing*, on the dial surface is a sign of age (and authenticity).
* Painted dials can fade or become worn. Repainted figures and signature are acceptable, but a damaged ground requires restoration.
* Painted metal dials may be scratched or chipped around the winding holes, due to careless use of the key.

Enamelled dials
Enamelled dials consist of enamel fired on top of thin copper sheet. They are prone to chipping and cracking. Restoration of cracked enamel is a specialized art, but may be called for if a clock is important or valuable. Avoid any clock with a heavily cracked or indented enamel dial. Slight chipping around the winding holes and some fine crazing over the dial surface is usually acceptable.

Hands
Although early lantern clocks have only one hand (for hours), from c.1660 most clocks have separate hour and minute hands. Some also have a centre seconds hand, although it is common to show seconds on a *subsidiary dial*. Hands are usually made of blued steel, although gilded brass is found from c.1790, particularly on the Continent of Europe. Until c.1740, the hour hand was often elaborate; the longer minute hand was simpler.
* Steel hands are "blued" by heating rather than painting. The process protects them and makes them easier to see; they will be a dark grey-blue colour.
* The hour hand is secured to a brass pipe projecting through the dial centre; the minute hand fits onto a concentric shaft in the centre of the pipe.
* Hands can break, usually through careless handling, but are easily repaired. If lost, a replacement in the correct style is acceptable. Hands are usually replaced for good reasons. However, they are a minor factor in judging authenticity.

CASES
The case houses the dial and the movement. Knowledge of case materials and fittings is useful in assessing the value and condition of a clock, as well as whether the case is contemporary with its dial and movement. In Britain and the United States, wooden cases predominate. Continental makers more commonly used metal, or combinations of materials.

Wooden cases
The wooden case was introduced c.1660 to house the movement, weights and pendulum used with the anchor escapement. The frame, or *carcass* of the long case is oak, overlaid with very thin layers of wood, or *veneers*. Original veneers are hand-sawed, and vary in thickness. Modern machine-sawed veneers are thin, and of uniform thickness. The most common woods are:
* *ebony*; a dense wood, dark when polished. It was used on early longcases c.1660-80, and on bracket clocks c.1660-1715.
* Pale fruitwoods were used if the case was to be *ebonized* (stained black). Ebonized cases are generally less desirable than ebony ones.
* *walnut*; an English wood used on most early longcases. Walnut can be very finely figured, depending how it is cut.
* *mahogany*; a dark wood imported from the Caribbean, and widely used c.1730-1840. Like walnut, mahogany can be finely figured. More modest pieces are paler, with a less pronounced grain. Makers in the United States often made use of local walnut or cherry, as a less costly alternative to mahogany.
* *oak* (solid, not veneered); used mainly by English provincial makers c.1710-1810.
* *rosewood*; a dark, strongly figured wood (often with black streaks), also imported. It was widely used in the early 19thC.

Decoration
Some of the finest late 17thC longcase and bracket clocks have veneers cut from the olive tree in rounded forms, known as "oyster" veneer.
* *Marquetry* – wood inlaid in decorative patterns – was popular on longcases in the late 17th and early 18thC. Early examples are ebony-veneered, with walnut standard from c.1680.

* *Lacquer* was fashionable from c.1710-60. Lacquered longcases may have a black, green, red or yellow ground, and tend to have Chinoiserie motifs painted over a *gesso* (raised work) ground, with extensive use of gold leaf; later examples may have applied prints. Lacquer is also found on bracket and tavern clocks.
* English bracket clock cases often feature *applied metal mounts*. These are usually brass (or, very rarely, silver). Some have an ornate metal top.
* *Brass inlay* is common on mahogany- or rosewood-veneered bracket clocks from the Regency period, and on some ebonized cases.
* French makers sometimes used *tortoiseshell*, or combinations of pewter, brass, tortoiseshell and wood veneer.

Metal cases
Brass is the most common metal. Although English lantern clocks have an all-brass case, metal cases are associated with French bracket and carriage clocks. All carriage clocks are brass-cased.
* Old brass is uneven, with marks left by the casting process. Modern rolled brass is of uniform thickness.
* Bronze was used on some English carriage clocks, and for the components of some French clocks.

Hinges and locks
Hinges and locks should always be original. If replacements, this may be evident from spare screw or pin holes, or from a "shadow" (outline) left by the original hinge. Gaps around the lock on the trunk door may indicate a replacement lock.

Condition
All clocks should have their original finish and decorative features intact. Some restoration is acceptable, if carried out sympathetically. Cases in need of extensive repair and reconstruction should be avoided. Changes in temperature and humidity cause veneers to lift and, on longcase clocks, for the trunk door to warp. All mouldings may loosen as the original glue dries out. On lacquered cases, bubbles may appear under the lacquer. This is caused by excessive heat and humidity. No clock should be kept in direct sunlight, as this causes the finish to bleach. Other problems include:
* missing finials
* damaged mouldings
* broken glass on the hood
* scratching or damage to polish.
* For condition of dial and movement, see appropriate entries above.

Woodworm
For woodworm, see p.59.

SIGNATURES
Most clocks are signed by the clockmaker. The signature can help to date a clock, but does not guarantee that a clock was made in the stated period, or by the man whose name it bears. During the 19thC, it was common for the clock to be signed by the retailer rather than the maker. The position of the signature varies with the type of clock, but usually appears on the dial and/or on the backplate.
* Cases were made separately, and are almost never signed.
* Occasionally, a fake signature has been added, usually to a clock that was not signed by its maker. One way to detect this is to feel the engraving; old engraving feels smooth, whereas new work can feel sharp.

CARE AND ATTENTION
Cases should be dusted from time to time, and polished regularly using a traditional wax polish. Cleaning of the movement should be left to a specialist clockmaker.
* Pivots, levers and some moving parts may be oiled sparingly with a proper clock oil. Never oil the wheels and pinions; oil attracts dust and dirt, increasing wear.

TRANSPORTING A CLOCK
The spring from which the pendulum is suspended is fragile, and may break when a clock is moved. Spring-driven clocks with a short pendulum, such as English bracket clocks or most 19thC French clocks should be held upright when carried. When transporting a bracket clock, take out the pendulum (if detachable), or pack the back with tissue paper. When transporting a longcase clock, remove the weights and pendulum. The hood should be taken off, and the dial and movement packed separately.

LANTERN CLOCKS

A lantern clock made c.1700 by John Knibb of Oxford

Taking its name from its similarity to a household lamp, the lantern clock was the earliest domestic clock to be produced in England. Its origins lie in the 16thC, with imported weight-driven Continental clocks, as well as with clocks made by immigrant clockmakers – often refugee Protestants – who settled in London in the late 16thC. Initially, all lanterns were made in London, but by the late 17thC a number of provincial makers had established themselves, most notably in Bristol and Oxford.

The production of London lantern clocks can be divided into three periods. The First Period (1580-1640) covers the establishment of the clock trade. During the Second Period (1640-60), clockmaking was disrupted by the English Civil

War (1642-49), but expanded rapidly after 1647. In the Third Period (1660-1700), the trade diversified, and variations such as miniatures were produced. In this period, the anchor escapement was introduced (see p.10)

All lantern clocks were originally weight-driven, struck the hours on a bell, and often featured an alarm mechanism. They are not accurate timekeepers, and typically lose or gain five to ten minutes each day.

The basic frame consists of a brass case on four short feet, with an engraved dial plate, three pierced frets, and strapwork and a single finial surmounting the characteristic top bell. With few exceptions, lantern clocks have one hand. Until the introduction of the arched dial in the 18thC, the construction and proportions of lantern clocks underwent only minor changes.

To allow the weights to descend, lantern clocks were always hung on the wall by means of an iron hoop and two locating spikes protruding from the bottom of the clock or the back feet. In some cases, the hoop and spikes were later removed, and the clock placed on an oak wall bracket.

Originally, all lantern clocks had a balance wheel escapement (see p.10) with two weights. These early clocks ran for 12 hours before requiring winding. However, this mechanism was inaccurate and required frequent adjustment. Almost without exception, from c.1680 lantern clocks were converted to a verge escapement (with a short pendulum), or to its successor, the more accurate anchor escapement (with a long pendulum). These versions were of 30-hour duration. In the 19thC, a revival of interest in lantern clocks led to the production of a spring-driven version, as well as to conversions of original lanterns to spring-driven mechanisms, with the weights removed. In the last 50 years, since lantern clocks became collectable, there have been some conversions back to a balance wheel. If a lantern clock has a balance wheel escapement, it will typically have one weight for the going train and another for the striking train. Examples with a verge or anchor escapement have a single weight. All lantern clocks are wound by means of an "endless rope" or chain (see p.45).

Lantern clocks began to go out of fashion by c.1700, and suffered a long period of neglect. It was only in the 19thC that collectors took an interest in them. Thus, it is very rare to find a lantern clock with all of its original parts. Without exception, all examples on the market today will have at least some replaced parts. Certain lantern clock parts, such as the frets, bell and bell straps, are detachable, and so have easily been lost over the centuries. Some replacement parts, such as side doors or backs, are acceptable. For more prominent parts, replacements must be carefully scrutinized. Replaced frets must be of extremely high quality. A lost hand is a major defect, but a well-finished replacement can be acceptable as long as the rest of the clock is in good condition. There are also a substantial number of fakes (see p.23), most produced during the 20thC.

EARLY LANTERNS

A First Period London lantern clock by Robertus Harue c.1602-14; ht 16in/41cm; value code C/D

Identification checklist for London lantern clocks
1. Is the clock brass throughout? (although some parts may be steel or iron)
2. Does it have a bell with a top finial?
3. Are there pierced frets around the top?
4. Does the chapter ring protrude from the sides?
5. Is there an alarm disc? (see below)
6. Is there a single prominent hand? (usually iron)
7. Are the holes in the baseplate slightly oval in shape? (rather than round)
8. Is the clock signed?

The London lantern clock: First Period (1580-1640)
The earliest English lantern clocks were produced by London makers. Although there is considerable variation in details, depending on the maker, lantern clocks are always made of brass, with pierced brass frets on the front and sides, a single hand, and a bell surmounted by strapwork and a finial. As they were designed to be hung on a wall, there is usually a hoop attached to the back, with two iron spikes – up to 2in/5cm in length – attached to the bottom of the backplate or the feet.

The signature
Most early lantern clocks are signed in the centre of the dial. It is unusual to find a lantern clock signed along the edge of the chapter ring, as on the example in the main picture.

Movements
Until the invention of the pendulum, all lantern clocks had a balance wheel escapement (see p.10). From c.1675, they were converted to a verge (with a short pendulum) or to an anchor escapement (with a long pendulum). Few examples with an original balance wheel have survived, although there have been some conversions back to balance wheel. Lantern clocks are all weight-driven, with one or two weights hung on ropes through holes in the bottom of the clock. Through wear, the holes are usually now more oval than round: a good sign of age.
* Early lanterns were wound twice daily.

Dials
Lantern dials are almost invariably brass. The applied chapter ring usually extends over the edges of the dial plate.

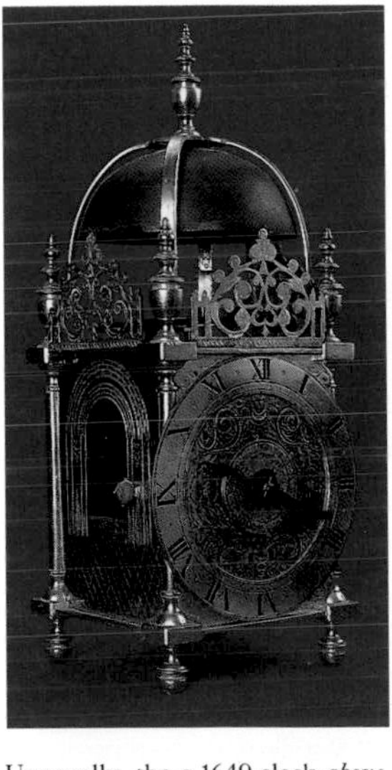

Unusually, the c.1649 clock *above* has a copper dial – probably unique to the anonymous maker. The narrow chapter ring is typical of early dials. On later lanterns (see p.20), it is wider.
* Geometric motifs, as on the dial of the clock in the main picture, were replaced by floral motifs from c.1615.
* London lanterns are typically 15-16in/38-41cm in height.

The alarm
The alarm disc in the dial centre is a common feature. The alarm is set by turning the disc until the tail of the hand shows the required hour. When this hour is reached on the chapter ring, a hammer strikes the bell. Alarms have often been removed in the process of conversion or repair. As long as the disc is in place, this is acceptable. The dial itself is engraved, but the area under the alarm disc was not. If the disc has been removed, the plain centre beneath will show.

The hand
The single hand is usually iron although there are some examples in brass.

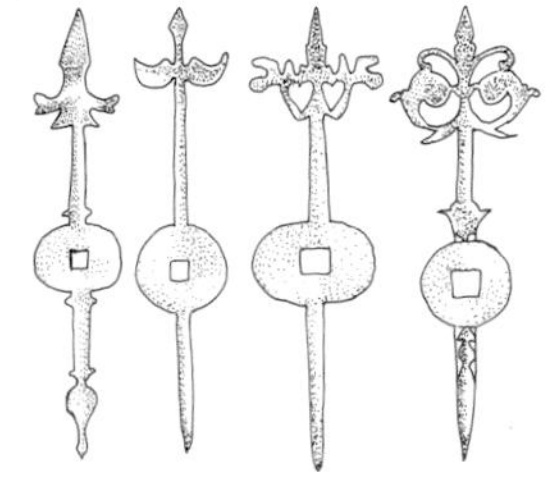

First Period hands, *far left* and *middle left*, are simple in shape. Hands from the Second Period, *middle right*, and the Third Period, *far right*, are elaborate.

Condition
Because of the number of fakes (see p.23) and reconstructions, any lantern clock should be examined carefully. A genuine example has worn pinions (see p.176), and the brass is of uniform patina. Replaced or faked parts appear brighter than the originals, or may be artificially distressed to look old. A lantern with all its original parts is rare, but some replacements are acceptable. On the clock in the main picture, these include the bell, frets, side door (visible) and alarm disc. Side doors have often been replaced.

LATER LANTERNS: 1

A Third Period London lantern clock by Joseph Lloyd c.1675; ht 14½in/37cm; value code D

Identification checklist for London and provincial lantern clocks from the Second and Third periods
1. Is the case brass, with an even patina? (indicating age)
2. Do frets feature dolphin, flower or peacock motifs?
3. Is there a narrow gap between the top of the front fret and the bottom edge of the bell?
4. Is the applied chapter ring wider than on early London lanterns? (see pp.18-19)
5. Does the clock have a single iron hand?
6. Is the clock hung using a "hoop and spikes" arrangement?
7. Are the arbors tapered without collets, or else (from c.1670) straight-sided with collets? (see below)
8. Is the clock signed? (probably on the dial)
9. On clocks with an arched dial, does the maker's signature appear in the arch?

Later London lantern clocks: Second (1640-60) and Third (1660-1700) periods
Later London lantern clocks share many characteristics with First Period lanterns. All are wall-hung. Frets have dolphin, leaf, flower or peacock motifs. Side frets may be engraved.
* If there is a wide gap or an overlap between the bell and the top of the frets, either the bell or the frets may be replacements. A replaced bell is more acceptable than replaced frets.

Dating
On early lantern clocks, the arbors (see p.172) are tapered and the wheels are attached without a collet. From c.1670, arbors are straight-sided, with a brass collet around the base. Tapering is indicative of high quality.

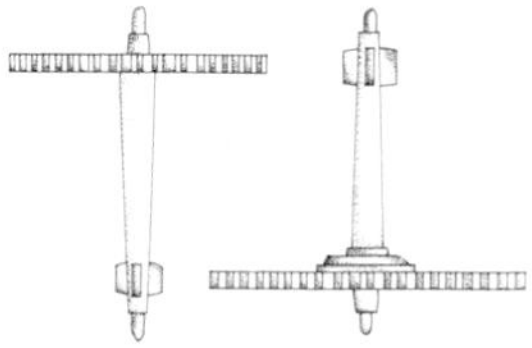

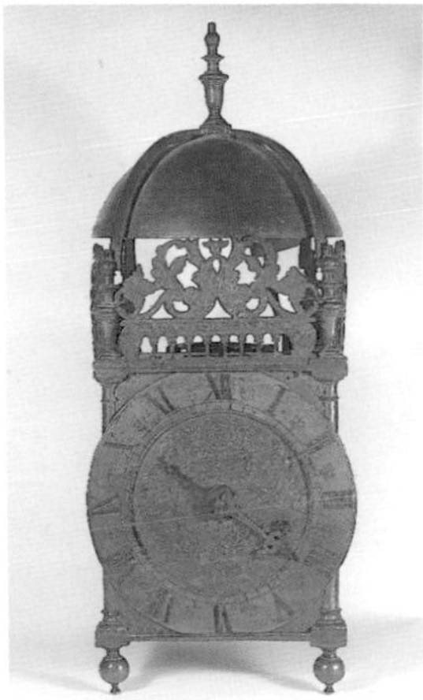

Because the dial centre on the clock *above* is engraved, it probably never had an alarm setting disc (which would have obscured the engraving). Made c.1655 by Richard Beck, the galleried fret indicates an early clock. A signed fret is rare; a signed dial is more usual.

Miniature lantern clocks
Miniature versions including travelling clocks, appeared from c.1670. Miniature clocks average 8-9in/21.6-24cm in height. They are often timepieces only, but most have an alarm.

Dials follow the pattern of standard size lanterns. On 18thC examples, like that shown *above*, made by Joseph Windmills c.1715, the wide chapter ring often has bold half-hour marks.
* All examples have a single hand, which should be intact; a good replacement is acceptable.

Collecting
There are few miniatures on the market. Those in good condition are highly sought-after. They should have an even patina. Be wary of any that look over-bright.
* Recent replicas are not intended to deceive, and look obviously new.
* For fakes see p.23.

19thC reproductions and conversions
Lantern clocks were also made during the 19thC. All are spring-driven, of eight-day duration and have a fusee (see p.11) or a French-made movement. Winding holes on the dial are a 19thC feature; original lanterns were wound by pulling up the weights.
* In the 19thC, many lanterns were converted to a spring-driven movement, with no weights.
* Victorian lanterns and conversions are substantially less valuable than the original clocks they were modelled on.

LATER LANTERNS: 2

Provincial lantern clocks
Lantern clocks were initially more common in London than in the provinces. However, as lanterns were relatively inexpensive to own, most provincial towns eventually had at least one maker. Cities such as Bristol and Ipswich became important centres for the production of lantern clocks. Provincial makers used the same materials and principles of construction as London makers.

Very unusually, this lantern clock, *above*, made with an anchor escapement, by the Staffordshire maker Samuel Stretch, was fitted in a long oak case (removed for this photograph). Because most of the clock was covered by the case, only the dial has been polished, accounting for the variation in patina between the dial and the rest of the clock.
* The minute hand and minute ring on this clock are rare: most lanterns show only the hours and quarter-hours, and have one hand.
* The large gap between the bell and the fret may indicate a replaced part. The bell should be just above the fret top (see p.20).

Engraved above Samuel Stretch's signature, the date of manufacture of the clock shown left is visible, *above*, although it would normally have been covered by the applied brass chapter ring. This is an exceptional feature: it is very rare to find a date on a lantern clock, or on any antique clock.

All lantern clocks have two side doors (often replaced) to provide access to the movement and to the winding rope or chain, and to keep out dust. On the example shown *above*, produced by an unknown South Lancashire maker c.1720, the handles to the side doors are clearly visible. On most lantern clocks, they are hidden by the protruding edges of the chapter ring.
* Unusually, the top straps on this clock run under rather than over the bell.

Lantern clocks by East Anglian makers, like the example shown *above*, made by William Rayment of Stowmarket, Suffolk, c.1730, were fitted with an anchor escapement, rather than converted from verge (see p.18). Lanterns remained popular in East Anglia until the late 18thC.

Replacement parts
Many lantern clock parts were detachable, and so have tended to be lost over the centuries. Certain replacement parts, such as side doors or backs, are acceptable. For more prominent parts, replacements must be carefully scrutinized: replaced frets must be of high quality. A lost hand is a major defect, but a well-finished replacement can be acceptable if the rest of the clock is in good condition.

Fakes
The lantern clock has been fairly extensively faked in the 20thC. Some fakes have been assembled from original parts, but there are others made from modern parts. Because of its all-metal construction, the lantern clock is the easiest clock to fake, as it requires only the skills of an engraver and a clockmaker. Metal cases are easier to age artificially than are wooden ones.

Arched-dial lantern clocks
The final stage in the development of the lantern clock, the arched dial, appeared c.1750. These were made almost exclusively by provincial makers, although some were produced in London for the Turkish market. The maker's signature usually appears in the arch, which is typically engraved, or has applied spandrels. All arched-dial lanterns are wall-hung. If stood on a table, the feet would not be visible, as the dial plate will usually be flush with the surface. All examples have feet. Later provincial arched-dial lantern clocks may lack the strapwork above the bell that is so characteristic of London lantern clocks. Instead, the bell may be fixed to a support or stand.
* Side doors are of the lift-out type, and are held in place by pin "hinges".

Many arched-dial lantern clocks have an anchor escapement (see p.10), but travelling clocks may have a verge escapement, with a short pendulum. All are of 30-hour duration. They include travelling alarm clocks, like the 4⅞in/12cm-high example shown *left*, made by the London maker William Allam c.1755. An original carrying case and weights, as shown with this clock, are rare features, adding greatly to value.

LONGCASE (TALLCASE) CLOCKS

A walnut-veneered longcase clock with pagoda top and finials by John Brentford c.1730

The longcase clock is the classic English clock, and is generally considered the finest achievement of English clockmaking. Longcases are prized by collectors for the high quality of their cases and movements, and enjoy a wide popularity today. There are large numbers in circulation, as they were possibly the most widely produced type of English clock. They were also produced in the United States – where they are known as tallcases – and on the Continent of Europe, but generally in lesser quantities than in England.

The earliest English longcase clocks were produced by London makers. By c.1700, longcases were being made by provincial clockmakers in centres such as Bristol and Oxford. By the early 18thC, clockmaking had become established throughout Great Britain, and even small villages could boast of having their own maker.

The long wooden case was an attractive but also practical solution to the problem of providing a stable, dust-free environment for the pendulum and the weights hanging below the clock movement. The basic frame, or carcass, is almost invariably oak. The earliest cases were veneered with ebony or ebonized wood. Later cases feature marquetry, walnut or mahogany veneers, lacquerwork and solid oak. As larger and more elaborate cases were produced, makers often made use of decorative touches such as top finials, pierced frets and brass stringing or mounts. In the United States, movements and dials imported from England were often fitted to cases made from local woods such as cherry or maple, or from more expensive imported mahogany.

The longcase movement consists of an anchor escapement with a long, seconds-beating pendulum (see p.10). The anchor escapement was considerably more accurate than its predecessor, the verge escapement, used in some very early longcases. The basic longcase movement changed little between c.1660, when the long pendulum was first applied to clocks, and c.1840, when the provincial longcase began to decline as a result of competition from inexpensive clocks imported from the United States and Germany. However, the longcase mechanism gradually incorporated complex mechanical refinements such as moon dials or astronomical or musical work. All examples are weight-driven, with the weights descending inside the case. Longcase clocks generally run for eight days before needing to be wound.

Dials were originally square in shape, but from c.1720 the arched dial became the most common style. The round dial came into fashion in the late 18th and early 19thC. The dial may be brass – either one-piece, or with an applied chapter ring – or else painted metal. The development of case and dial styles can be clearly followed and has been well recorded. A knowledge of cases, dials and hands is essential in dating any longcase clock and assessing authenticity.

In many instances, longcase clocks by provincial makers are the equal of their London counterparts, and provincial makers often produced interesting variations on the basic London styles. A number of country clocks with oak cases are of 30-hour, rather than eight-day duration. These 30-hour clocks, with either a brass or a painted dial, are sought-after today, as they represent the most inexpensive, yet still desirable, longcase timekeeper available on the market.

There is a large amount of information available on longcase clocks and their makers, which may help collectors check the provenance of a clock they are thinking of buying, and may also help with recognition and dating. The records of some important makers have also survived. Although almost all clocks are signed by the clockmaker, nothing is so far known about the craftsmen who made the cases.

The most collected longcase clocks today are mahogany-veneered examples by London makers. These were the standard good quality domestic clock during the second half of the 18thC, and significant numbers are still available. Experts consider the very early examples, especially those with ebony, walnut or marquetry cases, to be the most important English longcases. The superb workmanship and fine proportions of these clocks, particularly those by Thomas Tompion, Joseph and John Knibb and Edward East, make them the most highly sought-after – and expensive – longcase clocks.

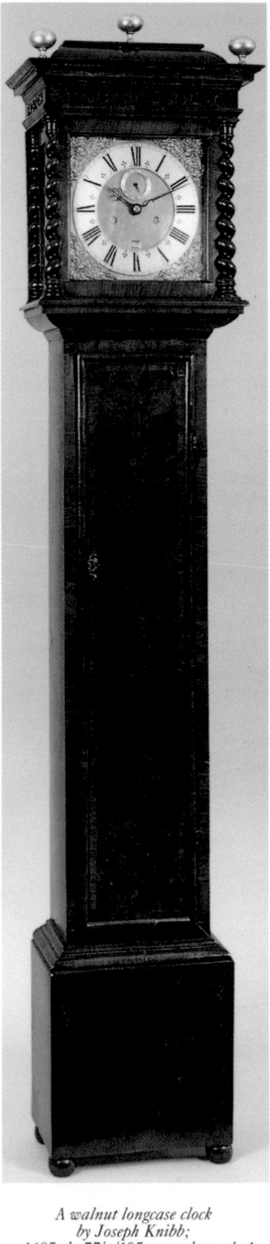

A walnut longcase clock by Joseph Knibb; c.1685; ht 77in/195cm; value code A

Identification checklist for early walnut longcase clocks, c.1665-c.1700
1. Is the case walnut?
2. Is there a shallow caddy top with finials? (some have cresting or a flat top)
3. Is the case about 77in/195cm in height?
4. Is the back crude?
5. Is the carcass oak?
6. Does the clock have a square brass dial, with an applied chapter ring and spandrels?
7. Is the dial centre "matted"? (see below)
8. Does the clock have an anchor escapement?
9. Is the pendulum a steel rod, with a brass-faced bob?
10. Is the dial signed?
11. Are the hands blued steel?

Early walnut longcases
The application of the long pendulum to clockmaking during the 17thC led to the development of the long case. This permitted the movement, weights and pendulum to be housed in a sturdy, dust-free enclosure. In England, the production of longcase clocks in walnut-veneered cases began c.1665, and was largely confined to London. The same clocks were also made with an ebony-veneered case (see right) c.1675-85, also by London makers, although in much smaller numbers. These clocks are rare and command extremely high prices today.

The case
The basic carcass was oak, over which walnut (or ebony) veneers were applied. Olivewood was sometimes used to create a distinctive circular, "oyster" pattern. "Oyster" cases are rare and very desirable.
* Longcase clocks are wound through the dial. On early examples, the hood was raised and secured on a catch to permit winding. Many hoods were

altered during the early 18thC, so that they slid forward. Doors were added at a later date. Such conversions should not lower the value of a clock.

Most clocks have a flat pediment supported by twist columns. Many also had a carved cresting secured by pegs to the hood, or a shallow caddy top with finials. On the example *above*, made by Joseph Knibb c.1685, the cresting has survived, but on others it has been lost or replaced. If lost, there may be holes in the hood to take the fixing pegs, or a "shadow" left by the original cresting. If replaced, the wood may not match, and the outline may not line up with the shadow left by the original.

Condition
Early longcase clocks typically had bun feet, fixed by pegs to holes in the base. Because they often stood on wet stone floors, the feet suffered damage and many were removed. Almost no original bun feet have survived, but as long as restored feet are sympathetic to the original, they do not affect the value of a clock.

Movements
Apart from a few early clocks with a verge escapement, all longcases were fitted with an anchor escapement (see p.10) and a long pendulum. They are usually of eight-day duration. Even when case styles changed, there were few changes to the movement. The pendulum is almost invariably a steel rod with a brass-faced bob. There are two brass-cased lead weights (one for the going train, and one for the striking train). All early longcases strike the hours on a bell.

* Longcases from this period rarely have their original winding crank and key. Loss of crank or key does not affect value; replacements can be obtained.

Beware
On some longcases, the bracket which secured the movement to the backboard may have been replaced. The holes in the backplate should line up with the hole in the backboard or with the remaining half of the bracket. If they don't, the movement may be a replacement, possibly intended to make the clock seem older than it really is. A replaced movement drastically reduces the value of a clock and any such examples should be avoided.
* For fakes and replaced movements, see p.59.

The dial
All early longcase clocks have a 9- or 10-inch square brass dial, with a narrow applied and silvered chapter ring and applied spandrels in the corners. The dial centre is brass but the surface is matted (roughened so that it appears hammered). Numerals are engraved and filled with black wax.
* Hands are blued steel; the hour hand may be elaborately pierced.
* By the 1690s, some examples are signed on the chapter ring rather than below it.

The contrast between dark ebony veneer and the brass dial, as shown on the clock *above*, produced c.1678 by Peter Knibb, made ebony veneer popular c.1665-80. The skeletonized dial on this clock is a rare feature. The chapter ring is cut away to reveal the matted surface.

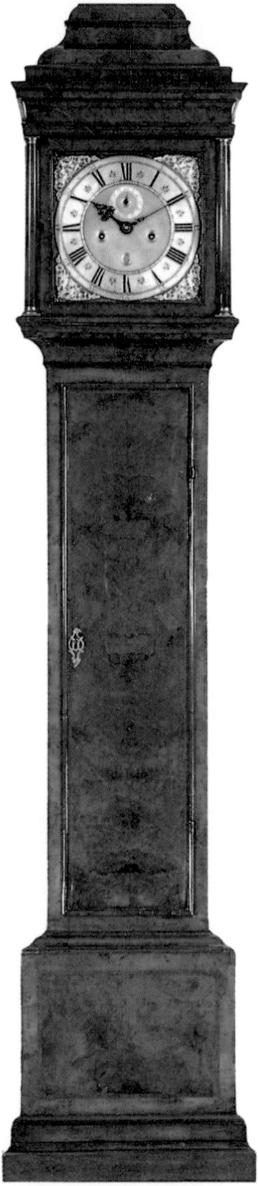

A walnut longcase clock with steep caddy top by Daniel Quare; c.1710; ht 94in/239cm; value code A

Identification checklist for later walnut longcase clocks (c.1700-60)
1. Does the clock have a caddy top, possibly with two or three finials?
2. Is there any pierced fretwork to the hood?
3. Does the case have a double-plinth base?
4. Is there a long, seconds-beating pendulum?
5. Does the clock have a brass dial, with applied chapter ring and spandrels?
6. Is the carcass oak?
7. If there is an arched dial, is there also a subsidiary dial or a strike/silent indicator in the arch?
8. Is the clock signed on the dial by the maker?
9. Are the hands made of blued steel?

Later walnut longcases
After the end of the 17thC, the design of walnut-veneered longcase clocks changed. New features included brass or wood top finials, pierced fretwork, or, as on the clock in the main picture, a caddy top. Size increased to accommodate 11- and 12-inch square or arched dials, and some clocks reached 103in/261cm in height. The sturdier double-plinth base reflects this increased size.
* The longcase movement (see p.27) did not change; later walnut longcases are typically of eight-day duration, strike the hours on a bell, and have an anchor escapement (see p.10).

The case
The figuring of the walnut veneer, laid over the standard oak carcass, varies greatly depending on how it was cut. Crossbanded veneers – laid in short sections at right angles to the main veneer – contribute to the desirability of a clock. The caddy top, which became increasingly common during the 18thC, may be steep, as on the clock in the main picture, or else fairly shallow.

Square dials
On square-dial walnut longcases, the chapter ring is more elaborate than on the early walnut and ebony veneered clocks (see pp.26-7), with a more prominent five-minute ring. Spandrels tend to be more elaborate, and the dial plate itself may be engraved. The signature is on the chapter ring or in the dial centre.
* There may be decorative rings around the winding holes.

Until 1700, the moulding directly under the hood was convex. After this date, the moulding is concave, as the unusual yew-veneered clock *above*, made by Richard Street c.1700, clearly shows. This shape is a reliable way of dating early longcase clocks. Very few longcases were made with yew veneer.
* The half-hour marks tend to be quite pronounced, and often end in a Maltese cross or *fleur-de-lys*.
* The pierced wooden "sound frets", backed with silk, allow the sound of the bell to escape. Fretwork is typical of longcases from this time. Side frets, as on the example above, are indicative of high quality. Replaced frets tend to be plain wood, and crudely cut.

Arched dials
The earliest arched-dial longcases appeared c.1715. The first arches were shallow, but they later became quite steep. The arch usually contains spandrels, applied around a strike/silent dial (see p.12), signature boss, calendar dial or the phases of the moon. The chapter ring usually has an inner quarter-hour ring.

The pagoda top with brass finials, like that shown *above*, from an arched-dial longcase made by John Ellicott c.1760, was common in the 18thC, although the caddy top was more usual.
* Brass finials are polished or gilded. Some finials are gilded wood. Finials are fragile; many have been lost.

The arched hood on the clock *above*, made by Joseph Windmills c.1715, is very rare, and is peculiar to this maker.
* The signature is engraved on a brass plate in the centre, rather than on the chapter ring.

MARQUETRY LONGCASES: 1

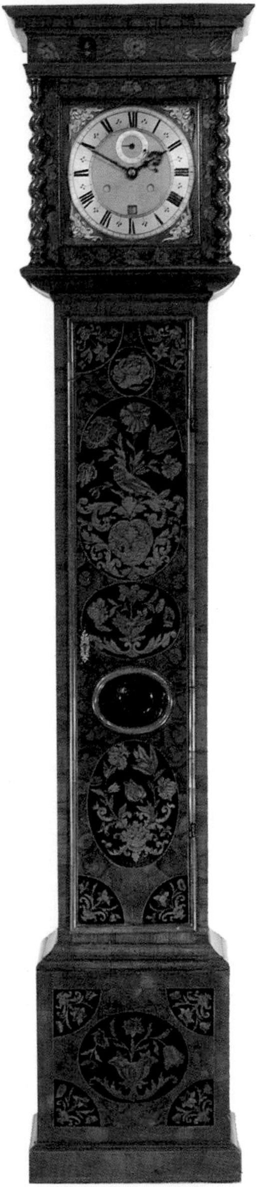

An early marquetry longcase clock by Charles Gretton; c.1680; ht 77in/195.5cm; value code A

Identification checklist for marquetry longcase clocks with 10-inch dials

1. Is the case walnut-veneered over an oak base?
2. Does it feature numerous small, distinct marquetry panels, with birds and flowers, or geometric patterns?
3. If the case has bun feet, are these original, or, if not, are there signs of the original feet? (see p.27)
4. Does it feature a lenticle?
5. Is the movement secured to the backboard by means of a bracket?
6. Are the sides plain, or crossbanded and strung? (more desirable than plain)
7. Is the dial brass with an applied chapter ring and spandrels?
8. Is there a maker's signature on the dial?
9. Are the hands made of blued steel?

Early marquetry longcases
The use of highly decorative patterns of inlaid veneer, known as marquetry, first became fashionable on the Continent of Europe, where Dutch and Flemish craftsmen produced some of the finest examples of marquetry furniture. Longcase clocks decorated with marquetry began to appear in England c.1680, but the fashion lasted only until c.1710, by which time decoration had become extremely lavish (see pp.32-3). Improvements in marquetry cutting techniques allowed makers to cover larger areas. The earliest examples held a 10-inch dial, and were very similar in design to walnut 10-inch dial longcases (see pp.26-7.). The dial invariably has an applied engraved and silvered chapter ring, a matted centre, applied spandrels and pierced blued steel hands.

Woods
The base veneer of marquetry longcase clocks is almost always walnut, which was laid over the standard oak carcass. On some of the earliest 10-inch dial clocks, the marquetry consisted of various coloured woods let into a background of ebony or ebonized wood. As on the very early clock shown in the main picture, the panels tend to be small and quite numerous, forming corner spandrels and oval reserves on the base and trunk. Inlaid panels most commonly follow a naturalistic pattern known as "bird and flower", and show a bird surrounded by elaborate leaves and flowers. On some cases, this marquetry foliage is stained green.

Beware
The marquetry on the base of the clock should always match that on the trunk door. Any obvious inconsistency in the appearance of the marquetry indicates that the case may have undergone repairs or alterations.

Movements
Marquetry longcases are typically of eight-day duration, with an anchor escapement and a long pendulum, and strike the hours on a bell. Some early clocks, like the one in the main picture, which strikes the quarter-hours on two bells, have mechanical refinements.
* The movement is secured by means of a bracket (see p.27).

Hoods
Like early walnut longcases, early marquetry longcases tend to have a flat top, although some are embellished with simple cresting. A convex moulding below the hood indicates a clock made before 1700 (see p.29).
* The marquetry flowers across the top of the hood of the clock in the main picture are an unusual, individualistic touch. Pierced frets are more common.
* The twist columns are very typical of many early English longcase clocks.

Condition
Original marquetry has an undulating surface, caused by the shrinkage of the boards underneath the veneer. If it has a smooth, even surface, it may be a recent replacement.

Parquetry
Inlay of more geometric pattern, using contrasting veneers and known as parquetry, is found on some early inlaid clocks.

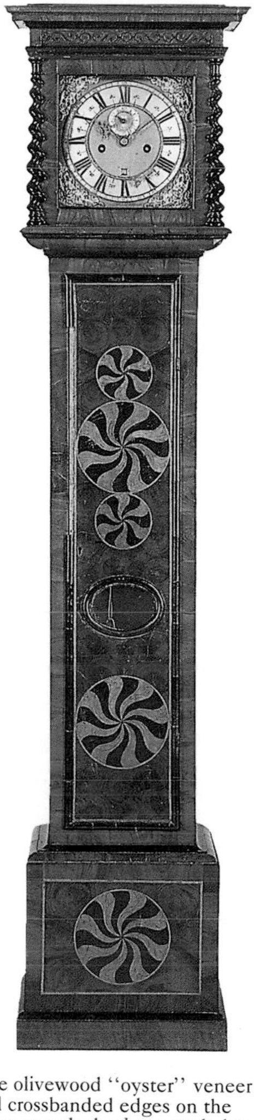

The olivewood "oyster" veneer and crossbanded edges on the parquetry clock *above*, made by William Cam, are indicative of a piece of the finest quality.
* The oval glass window in the centre of the trunk door, known as a lenticle, was a popular feature during the 17th and early 18thC. It allowed the pendulum to be seen to swing regularly.

MARQUETRY LONGCASES: 2

A marquetry longcase clock by Peter Mallett; c.1695; ht 82in/208cm; value code A

Identification checklist for later marquetry longcases with 11- and 12-inch dials
1. Is the marquetry either in panels or all over the surface of the case?
2. Does the clock have a caddy top?
3. Are there any brass finials on top of the hood?
4. Does the hood slide forward?
5. Is the dial brass, with an applied chapter ring and spandrels?
6. Is there a lenticle?
7. Is the clock signed?

Later marquetry longcases
The production of marquetry longcase clocks reached its peak during the 1690s and early 1700s. The makers were chiefly London-based. However, there are also some fine examples by provincial makers. Cases tend to be large in size – typically around 90in/228cm – and were intended to accommodate 11- and 12-inch square brass dials.

Movements
Most marquetry longcases are of eight-day duration, with an anchor escapement and a long, seconds-beating pendulum. All examples strike the hours on a bell. In the 1670s, the development of "rack" striking (see p.12) made it possible to incorporate refinements to the striking train. The clock in the main picture strikes the half-hours in addition to the hours. Other clocks may strike the quarter-hours instead.

Dial
The square dial is always brass, with an applied silvered chapter ring and applied spandrels in the corners of the dialplate. There is virtually always a seconds dial and a calendar aperture.

Marquetry
Later marquetry longcase clocks tend to feature more extensive and more elaborate inlay than on early examples. Crossbanding of woods and decorative stringing is

typically of very high quality. The "bird and flower" pattern appears on many of the 11-inch dial examples as well. As on the clock in the main picture, marquetry panels tend to be larger and fewer in number than on earlier marquetry cases (see pp.30-1).

On 12-inch dial marquetry longcases, the inlay typically covers the whole surface of the case, instead of being confined to small panels on the trunk door and base as before. Although the clock *above*, made by John Westoby c.1700, follows the "bird and flower" pattern, inlay is often more abstract. Other marquetry patterns include:

* Scroll (or Arabesque); abstract, symmetrical foliage with some figures; usually on a dark ground
* Seaweed; intricate foliage, but with no strapwork or figures.

The case
The caddy top, often covered with marquetry and flanked by brass finials, replaced the earlier flat pediment on many 11- and 12-inch dial clocks. Flat pediments appear on some 11-inch dial clocks, but on others a flat pediment indicates that cresting or a caddy top has been removed.

The plain hood columns, elaborate gilded trunk mounts and gilded, carved wood finials on the 12-inch dial clock *above*, all indicate a clock from the later part of the marquetry period. Produced c.1700 by the London maker Henry Harper, the case of this example features all-over Arabesque marquetry.
* The twist columns characteristic of 17thC hoods were used on some later marquetry longcases.
* The hood generally slides forward rather than upward, to provide access to the dial and movement. It is very uncommon to find a rising hood in a 12-inch dial clock made after the beginning of the 18thC.
* In order to fit the very long case of these clocks into a modern room (which usually has a lower ceiling), the characteristic double-plinth base may have been shortened to a single plinth.

MAHOGANY LONGCASES: 1

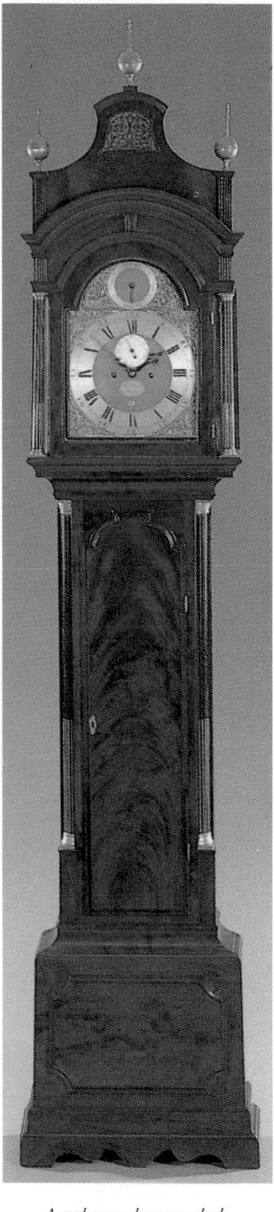

A mahogany longcase clock by Alexander Cumming; c.1780; ht 98in/249cm; value code D

Identification checklist for mahogany longcase clocks
1. Does the clock have a pagoda top? (The best quality examples have an arched top with a single plinth and finial)
2. Is the case mahogany?
3. Is the brass dial arched? (with an applied chapter ring and spandrels)
4. Does the clock have a double-plinth base?
5. Is the base panelled?
6. Are there any quarter-columns (perhaps brass-strung)?
7. Are there any free-standing columns to the hood? (The best quality examples have chamfered, reeded corners, often with brass stringing)
8. Does the clock have a long pendulum and a matching pair of brass-cased weights?
9. Is it signed on the dial?
10. Are the hands blued steel?

Mahogany longcase clocks
Mahogany veneer was used by London casemakers from c.1740. Longcase clocks with mahogany cases are of very good quality, and were produced in large numbers c.1750-1810. Nearly all are of eight-day duration and strike the hours on a bell. The clock in the main picture has a form of anchor known as a dead beat (see p.173).

The case
The basic carcass is oak covered with mahogany veneer. Cases with pronounced figuring are the most desirable. Like the clock in the main picture, mahogany longcases often feature an elaborate pagoda top, usually with two or three brass "ball and spire" finials. Sometimes, a pagoda top has been removed to reduce the height of the clock. A "shadow" on the top of the hood

indicates where the top once stood. Clocks with an arched top also have a pierced cresting. There are some architectural tops. Finials should be intact and original.

* Mahogany longcases often have quarter-columns, sometimes with brass stringing, at the corners of the trunk and base. The hood columns are usually free-standing. Instead of quarter-columns, others have either plain or chamfered and reeded corners. Any intact brass stringing is a desirable feature.

Dials

The great majority of mahogany longcases typically have an arched 12-inch dial, with applied chapter ring and spandrels in the corners of the dial plate and the sides of the arch. 11-inch arched dials are very rare. There are no half- or quarter-hour marks on the chapter ring.

The one-piece silvered and engraved dial, as shown *above*, is an important variation produced c.1800 in London by the well-known Vulliamy family. Silvered and engraved brass dials were introduced c.1760, but were used on longcase clocks for only a few years. Vulliamy pieces often have square dials, and these have an architectural top, as shown above, rather than a pagoda top with finials. Unusually, Vulliamy clocks have a serial number, and can be accurately dated, by referring to the maker's records, which have survived.

* The signature on a mahogany longcase is always engraved. It may appear across the centre of the dial, as shown above, on the chapter ring or on a silvered brass plaque applied to the dial.

Recognition point

Mahogany longcases typically feature a panelled base on a double plinth, which may be plain or shaped.

The finest quality pieces, like the clock *above*, made c.1780 by the noted maker John Holmes (see pp.36-7), also have quarter-columns to the base. Top frets, like those above the dial on this example are usually made of cast brass or wood.

* Side frets may be of wood or brass. There may be a pierced fret in the centre of the hood between the finials. Wooden frets are extremely fragile, and replacements do not affect value.

The finest mahogany longcases
The best London mahogany longcases were made by Thomas Mudge Sr, William Dutton and John Holmes, c.1770-1805. These clocks are more sought-after than those by other London makers. Mudge and Dutton were in partnership 1759-90. (For checklist, see p.34).

Clocks by the best makers differ from the standard London mahogany case mainly in the treatment of the top. As on the example *below left*, signed by Vigne but with a movement by Holmes, the top is arched, with a single plinth and finial in the centre. Chamfered, reeded corners, sometimes with brass stringing, take the place of freestanding hood columns. The hood door may be of plain rectangular section, or else, in the best examples, concave.
* The clock shown left is signed below the centre of the dial. The maker's signature may also be on the chapter ring.

Beware
The single plinth to the hood is a typical feature of mahogany longcases by the best London makers. It may have been removed because of damage during use or to reduce the height of the clock. A "shadow" on top of the hood (see p.27) indicates whether a particular piece once had a plinth. The finial is usually a brass ball, either plain or pierced. On some pieces, the finial has been lost.

Dials
The clock shown left has a one-piece engraved silvered dial, but others have an applied brass chapter ring with spandrels.
* Good quality engraved and silvered dials usually survive largely free of cracks and crazing.

Movements
Movements are identical with those of other longcases. They are of eight-day duration, with an anchor escapement. All examples strike the hours on a bell.

Condition
Due to changes in humidity, longcases are vulnerable to warping, particularly the trunk door. Warping of the door is more obvious at the top – at eye level – than at the bottom. A warped door can be remedied through rehanging: the hinges must be repositioned. Repairs are acceptable, as a warped door is likely to be original.

Cases
Mudge, Dutton and Holmes favoured high quality cases, with strongly figured mahogany veneer. The interior will be planed, but not polished or veneered. Backs are unplaned.

Even on the best quality mahogany longcases, such as the classic Mudge and Dutton clock, *above*, made c.1780, the panelling on the trunk door and base is similar to the standard mahogany longcase. The shallow pad feet are characteristic; some cases have four pads, others only two. The two pads enable the clock to lean slightly back against the wall, improving its stability.
* The arched door panel is a typical feature.

Pendulums
A characteristic feature of clocks made by Holmes is the use of a wood-rod regulator pendulum. Wood is less susceptible than steel to changes in temperature, which can alter the length of a steel pendulum rod and thus affect its accuracy. The bob consists of a large disc made of lead, with a smaller spherical brass bob suspended underneath, as shown *left*. The small brass bob offers a choice of six settings, adjusted to achieve fine regulation. The wood-rod regulator pendulum was fitted on almost all longcases made by Holmes. In some cases, it may have been replaced by a more durable standard steel rod with brass-faced lead bob.

The date dial on the clock *above* makes it possible to date it to after c.1790, when the date dial replaced the calendar aperture. This clock was made by Johnson of Gray's Inn Passage; and is a rare (and slightly less valuable) example of a maker adopting Holmes's style.

A painted-dial mahogany longcase clock by Grove; c.1800; ht 93in/236cm; value code D

Identification checklist for painted-dial mahogany longcases

1. Does the clock have either a pagoda or a plain arched top?
2. Does the base have a double plinth?
3. Is the base panelled?
4. If it has an arched dial, does the clock also have freestanding hood columns and a shaped apron base?
5. Does it strike the hours?
6. Are the weights brass-cased? (clocks by London makers only)
7. Is there a calendar dial?
8. Is the clock signed on the dial by the maker?
9. Are the hands made of blued steel?

Note
The checklist also covers painted-dial mahogany longcases by provincial makers (see p.40-1)

Painted-dial mahogany longcases (c.1780-1810)
The standard mahogany longcase features a brass dial with applied chapter ring and spandrels. However, painted dials – cut from iron sheet and painted white – were less expensive to produce than brass dials, and during the late 18thC, gradually replaced brass. Today, painted-dial longcases are not as valuable as those with brass dials, but fine examples do exist.

Dials
Arched dials are the most common, but round dials do turn up, especially on clocks by provincial makers (see right). Painted dials typically feature floral motifs, as well as historical scenes or personalities, such as Admiral Nelson, or mythological or allegorical figures such as the figure of Justice in the arch of the clock in the main picture. The numerals and signature are always written in black. The artists are not known. Painted dials should be in good

condition, but some restoration is acceptable.

* Clocks with arched dials tend to have shaped bases, and feature the same door shape and moulding as London mahogany longcases (see pp.34-5).
* The five-minute ring, like that on the dial of the clock in the main picture, disappeared by the end of the 18thC.

The falseplate
The dial of most longcase clocks is connected to the movement by riveted feet. However, because the dial and movement of painted-dial mahogany longcases were produced separately, the dial feet did not always line up with the holes on the frontplate, so many have an iron falseplate to secure the dial.

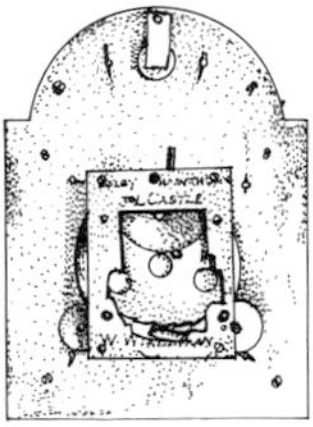

Without the addition of the falseplate, it would have been impossible to add new rivets to the dial after it had been painted. Before buying a clock, remove the hood to see whether it has a falseplate. If there is one fitted but there are still spare holes in the frontplate of the movement, the dial may not be original.
* The falseplate often gives the name of its maker. Many were produced in Birmingham.

Signatures
Because most examples have a calendar dial, the signature on later painted-dial clocks nearly always runs horizontally across the centre of the dial.

Hoods
The hoods of later mahogany longcases with arched dials tend to have freestanding columns on either side of the dial, and feature either a pagoda top with two finials, or an arched top with three finials. On round-dial examples, there are no hood columns. Some clocks were made with a plain arched top, but these are comparatively rare.

Occasionally, as in the example *above*, made by John Leplastrier c.1805, there is a carved (or pierced) cresting fixed to the hood between the finials.
* All painted-dial clocks strike the hours, and almost all have a seconds dial. Like this example, clocks made after c.1790 have a subsidiary calendar dial rather than a date aperture.

Although produced c.1800 by the London makers Dwerrihouse and Carter, this mahogany longcase with a round painted dial, *above*, is more typical of provincial designs, notably in its use of a satinwood fan inlay.
* Most London clocks (and some provincial ones) have lead weights cased in brass. Provincial clocks are likely to have plain lead or iron weights.

MAHOGANY LONGCASES: 4

Provincial mahogany longcases
Mahogany longcases by provincial makers are identical in many respects to those made in London, although there are distinctive regional features. These clocks were produced c.1750-1805, slightly later than London examples.

Liverpool
Because of its importance (as a seaport), Liverpool was also a major centre of clock production during the 18th and 19thC. One of the most significant Liverpool longcase makers was Joseph Finney (1708-72).

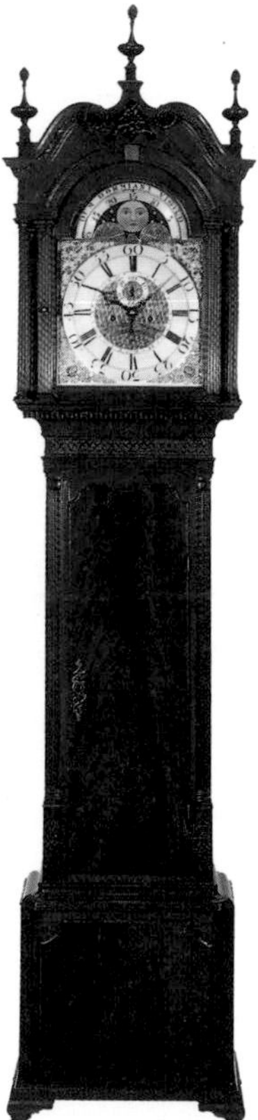

Provincial mahogany longcases tend to be large, with well-proportioned cases. The clock *above*, made by Scotson of Liverpool c.1770, reaches a height of 97in/246cm. The elaborate swan-necked top, with very fine carved finials, is a distinctive feature of Liverpool clocks: mahogany longcases more commonly have brass finials. The crosshatched dial centre is very unusual, particularly as the signature is simply engraved on a smooth area of the centre, rather than on an applied plaque.

Other typical Liverpool features include:
* bracket feet (also found on other provincial longcases)
* the reeded hood door and columns
* the painted moon dial in the dial arch, bearing the Latin inscription *DUM DORMIANT VIGILO* ("While you sleep I watch")
* a centre date hand
* the decorative fret in the centre of the hood top is made of a panel of *verre eglomisé* (reverse-painted glass). This feature is also common to clocks by other northern makers.

Dating point
The "blind" fret at the top of the trunk of the clock shown left is so-called because it is purely decorative and does not allow the sound of the bell to escape. Blind fretwork, also found on furniture of the period, indicates that the clock was made during the mid-18thC.

Edinburgh makers produced very distinctive cases: the swan's-neck pediment on the clock *above*, made by James Howden c.1795,

is a classic Edinburgh feature. Notable makers include:
* James Cowan (1744-81)
* Thomas Reid (1762-1809).

This spectacular clock, *above*, produced c.1780 by Moore of Ipswich, rivals the best London mahogany longcases. The dial not only features four subsidiary dials (day, month, strike/silent and tune selection) in the corners, but the musical movement plays seven tunes as the automata in the dial arch move. These features are unusual on a longcase. The brass frets, brass finials, quarter columns to the base and brass stringing all indicate a piece of the highest quality.

Other notable Ipswich makers include:
* Richard Duck (1711-62)
* Thomas Read (1733-1817).

Automata

Automata – mechanical figures operated by a concealed mechanism – are found on a few longcase clocks. Such clocks are rare and very costly. Automaton figures, often linked to musical work, are usually positioned in the dial arch. Subjects include musicians, as on the clock shown left, the phases of the moon, or a rocking ship. Clocks with automata should always be run first, to ascertain that the mechanical figures and musical work are still in working order: bells may be missing or wrongly replaced, and pins on the barrel may have broken off.
* On automaton clocks, a third winding hole on the dial is used to wind the automata and any musical or quarter striking work, in addition to holes for the going and striking trains.

This painted dial, *above*, signed by Robson of North Shields, is decorated to commemorate a local marriage. A painted "marriage dial" like this is very rare, and more likely to be found on a clock by a northern maker. North Shields is not otherwise known for clocks.

Value

London mahogany longcases fetch higher prices than provincial ones. A provincial clock may be a better purchase, as the quality may be high.

OAK LONGCASES: 1

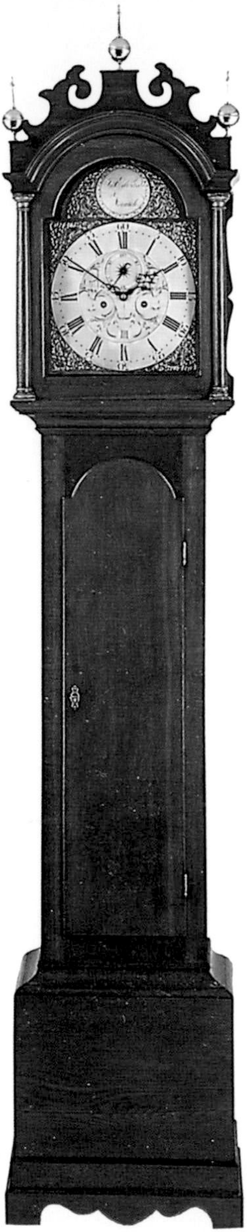

An oak longcase with an arched brass dial by John Edwards of Norwich; c.1780; ht 94in/239cm; value code D

Identification checklist for oak longcase clocks
1. Is the case plain, with little decoration except for freestanding columns on the hood?
2. Is there a caddy top?
3. Is the dial square (early 18thC) or arched (late 18thC)?
4. If it has a brass dial, is the clock of eight-day duration, or, if painted, is it of 30-hour duration? (Brass dial 30-hour clocks are rare; see p.45.)
5. Does the dial have an applied chapter ring and spandrels?
6. Are the weights lead or iron?
7. Are the hands blued steel?
8. Is the clock signed?

Oak longcase clocks
Produced in large numbers from c.1700-1800, oak longcase clocks with either brass or painted dials were made almost exclusively by provincial, rather than London, makers. Designs varied widely, and each region produced clocks with their own characteristics. The most distinctive pieces are by Scottish or East Anglian makers. Early oak longcases usually have a square dial. Few of these have survived in good condition. Arched-dial clocks, like the example in the main picture, are more common today.
* Oak is not valuable enough to have been faked. There are also few reproductions; mahogany has always been more fashionable. However, on some early pieces, a new dial or movement may have been substituted for the original one. Look for spare holes in the front plate of the movement, or winding arbors that do not line up exactly with the winding hole.

Movements
The movements of oak longcases are well-made, and often come up to the standards of London clocks. Weights are generally

made of lead or iron. Most examples on the market are of eight-day duration, although painted-dial oak longcases are commonly of 30-hour duration (see p.45).

Cases
On the earliest oak longcase clocks, the hood may be flat-topped. Both square and arched-dial versions usually feature freestanding hood columns on either side of the dial. With the exception of the hood, cases are usually undecorated, although on the trunk door there may be an elaborate escutcheon (the protective brass plate surrounding a keyhole). On early versions, the coarse-grained oak is generally of a rich, "mature" colour. Later, the oak is lighter, and more honey-coloured. Earlier oak longcases have a solid plinth base (single or double). Later cases may have a shaped base.
* East Anglian makers often added the kind of frilly cresting, known as a "whale's tail", shown on the piece in the main picture. Scottish makers often added a steep swan's-neck pediment above the arched dial, as well as a double "wave" shape to the top of the trunk door.

Oak longcases with square brass dials, like the example shown *above*, made c.1765 by Thomas Richardson of Weaverham, often feature a caddy top. This may have been cut to reduce the height of the clock.
* Dials have an applied chapter ring and spandrels. Hands are usually of pierced blued steel, with the hour hand the more elaborate.

Dating point
From c.1790, the calendar aperture, which appears on the Edwards example, as well as on many other oak longcases, was replaced by a calendar dial.

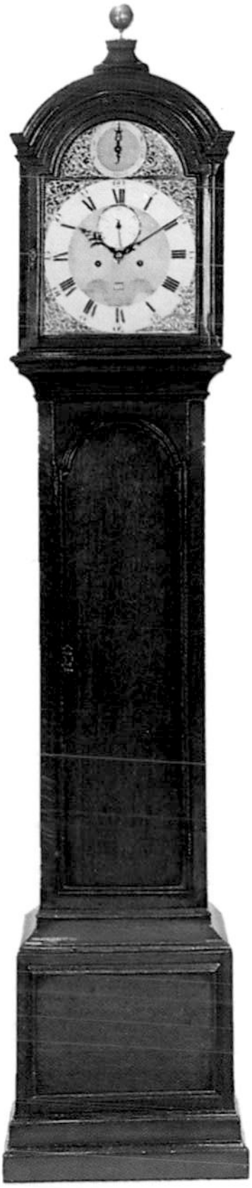

Oak longcases by London makers are unusual. The clock *above*, made by Thomas Haley c.1790, follows the style of Mudge or Dutton (see pp.36-7). It features the panelled base and trunk door, and single finial typical of their clocks.
* Oak longcases are always signed, either in the arch or on the dial. The clock shown above is signed on a plaque applied to the dial centre. On the clock in the main picture, the signature is in the arch, indicating the absence of a strike/silent lever.

OAK LONGCASES: 2

Painted-dial oak longcases
Oak longcase clocks with painted dials are essentially a provincial phenomenon, and were produced c.1800-40. The painted dial could be produced more inexpensively than applied brass or engraved and silvered brass dials. Painted-dial oak longcases were produced throughout England on a reasonably large scale. Even small town and village makers would have made these clocks, and there are a fairly large number still in circulation today.
* All examples are weight-driven, with an anchor escapement (see p.10) and a long, seconds-beating pendulum.
* For checklist, see p.42.

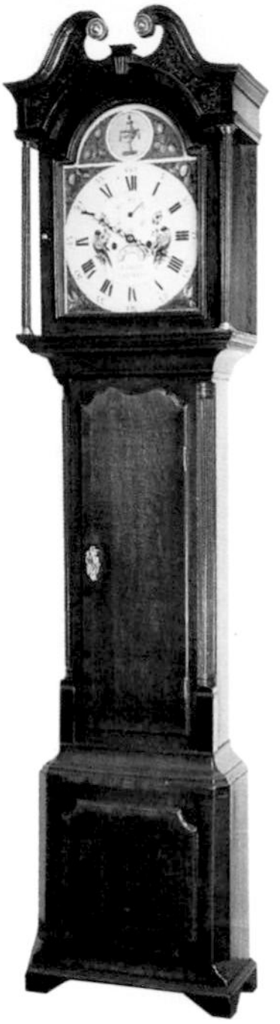

The swan's-neck pediment on the clock *above*, made by Benjamin Harlow of Lane End c.1795, was a common provincial feature. Oak pieces often have an elaborate escutcheon.

Unusually, the dial of the clock *above* features Arabic numerals and brass hands. This clock was produced c.1810 by Charles Raymond.

Dials are arched and appear identical to those of painted-dial mahogany longcases (see p.38-9). The arch may have a pastoral scene, as shown *above*, mythological or allegorical figures, or the phases of the moon. There are often painted flowers in the corners of the dial and in the arch. The extensive flowers, fruit and birds, as well as the elaborate hands on the dial of the Harlow clock shown left are indicative of high quality.

* The date aperture below the dial centre revolves on a wheel. The correct date is read against a central pointer.
* The dial is always signed.
* For the condition of painted metal dials, see p.15.

Thirty-hour clocks

Longcase clocks of 30-hour, instead of eight-day duration, were first made in the early 18thC, and were produced until c.1825. Cases were simple in style and usually of oak: mahogany cases are rare. Apart from some American wall clocks, 30-hour clocks are an English product. They were produced mainly in small towns.

Dials may be square or arched, and either brass or painted. The best ones have a calendar aperture, as on the clock shown *above*, made by the Yorkshire maker Thomas Hargreaves, c.1785.

* Cases may have a flat top or, on clocks with an arched dial, a swan's-neck pediment. Oak cases are usually in good condition, but the base may have been cut or the feet removed to fit the clock into a room with a lower ceiling.

Value point

Thirty-hour clocks were commonly known as "cottage clocks" because they were far less expensive for people of moderate means to purchase than were longcases of eight-day duration. Today, the 30-hour clock is the most affordable longcase for the collector.

Movements

Movements are more crudely made than those of an eight-day clock, although 30-hour clocks are accurate. They strike the hours on a bell, and have the single iron or lead weight typical of provincial clocks.

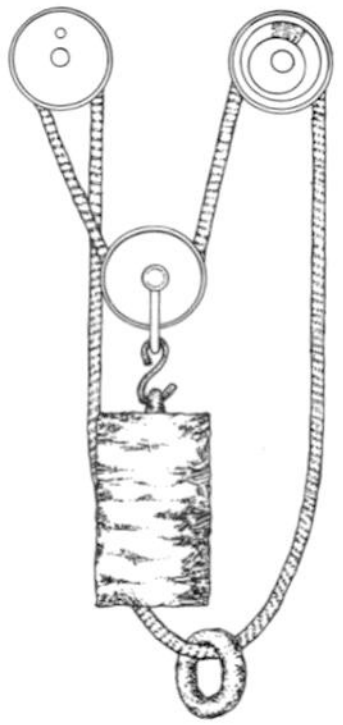

There are no winding holes on the dial of a 30-hour clock, because they are wound from inside the case by pulling on an "endless rope" or "endless chain" – a loop of rope running on a system of pulleys, *above*. The clock is wound by pulling on the rope, which raises the weight. The ring keeps the rope taut. The pull of the weight drives the top pulleys, which are linked to the wheel trains. Although these clocks were intended to be wound daily, they ran for 30 hours to allow "time in hand". The system was used on lantern clocks (see p.21), some wall clocks and a few Vienna regulators.

LACQUERED LONGCASES: 1

A lacquered longcase clock by Thomas Hally; c.1740; ht 95in/241cm; value code B

Identification checklist for lacquered longcase clocks with painted or applied print decoration
1. Is the dial square (before c.1740) or arched?
2. Is there a caddy or pagoda top?
3. Is the case decorated all over?
4. Does it show Chinoiserie or pastoral views?
5. Is the decoration on the door and base balanced and well drawn?
6. Are applied prints adhering soundly to the wood and free of bubbles?
7. Is the dial brass, with an applied chapter ring and spandrels?
8. Is there a double plinth base?
9. Are the hands blued steel?
10. Is the clock signed?

Early lacquered longcases (c.1700-40)
Longcase clocks with lacquer decoration – either traditionally painted or applied (see pp.48-9), were first made in quantity c.1730. Both types were produced mainly in London.
* Dials have an applied chapter ring and spandrels, and a calendar aperture (rather than a calendar dial).
* Lacquered longcases are usually of eight-day duration, with an anchor escapement and a long pendulum.

The case
Lacquerwork was usually painted or applied to an oak base, although pine was used for some early examples, and for later provincial cases. The base is usually an unshaped double plinth. Early pieces feature a square dial and caddy top; arched dials and pagoda tops are common on later examples. Finials are generally gilt-painted wood, as are the capitals on the pine hood columns.

Recognition point
The arched top of the trunk door on the clock in the main picture is a characteristic feature of Chinoiserie longcases made after c.1720.

Beware
If the case has a flat top, it has probably been cut: there are few flat-topped lacquered longcases. Similarly, there are few with arched tops, apart from those missing a pagoda top.

Decoration
Lacquer decoration covers the whole of the case. Chinoiserie motifs are painted on the trunk door and base over a layer of gesso. The rest of the case and hood are covered with painted gilt foliate motifs.

Painted Chinoiserie decoration on early lacquered longcases typically features scenes of pavilions, courtiers and foliage, as on the detail shown *above*.

Paint condition
Original ground colour is always faded. Areas of colours or gilding that do not blend well with the rest of the case may be restored. Bubbling under the lacquer can be restored, but the amount needing restoration should not be excessive.

* Painted decoration is executed over a gesso base, and may have come away in places.
* Pine hood columns are susceptible to attack by woodworm (see p.59).

Cases with a red ground, like the early painted example *above*, produced c.1705, are very rare. Black is the most usual ground colour, followed by green. A green ground can look black if the case has a heavy layer of wax and dirt.

Fakes
Fakes usually consist of new lacquer over an old case. A fresh surface may indicate recent work. Excessive crazing may mean artificial ageing.

Later lacquered longcases (c.1740-80)
Later Chinoiserie lacquered longcases typically have a pagoda top and an arched dial. As with the earlier types (see pp.46-7), the most valuable have a red ground. Green or black grounds are less valuable. Later lacquered longcases were made by most London makers, as well as by some provincial ones. They sometimes feature applied rather than painted decoration.

The pagoda top, as on the faded red ground clock shown *above*, tends to feature two or three gilt finials. Although the colour on this clock has faded, this is a desirable feature, as it is a sign of age – and of authenticity – that is hard to reproduce artificially. Unusually, this clock was not made in London, but was produced c.1780 by John Massingham of Fakenham.
* The centre seconds hand (rather than a seconds dial), is an unusual feature. In addition, the dial centre is silvered rather than matted (hammered).

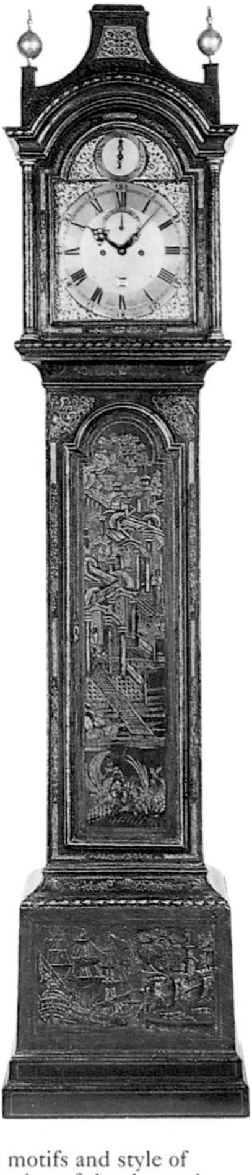

The motifs and style of execution of the decoration on the trunk door and base panel are often of standard composition. The ship motif on the base of the

clock shown *below left*, produced by John Monkhouse c.1770, is almost exactly the same as that on the base panel of the Massingham piece at left. This motif is found on only a few clocks, usually on the base.
* Instead of a strike/silent dial, the dial arch sometimes contains a signed metal boss.

Painted or applied?
The difference between painted Chinoiserie longcases and those with applied prints is that the prints are only on the trunk door and base panel. The rest of the case is decorated in gold leaf, with gold composition on the sides. Clocks with applied decoration are among the rarest lacquered longcases.

The subjects of applied prints were typically pastoral scenes, as shown on the detail *above*, from a clock by Joseph Millis, c.1765. As with all longcases of this type, the artists are unknown. Biblical scenes were popular, but are not sought after today.

Print condition
Applied prints should adhere completely to the surface of the lacquered case and be largely free of bubbles or lifting. Any applied prints should be original to the case, look as if they have always been there, and show the same signs of ageing throughout. Be suspicious of any lacquered longcase in which the different prints do not appear to be by the same artist, as this may indicate that the case has been altered at some point.
* For the condition of the carcass and of painted decoration, see p.47.

It is unusual to find a print-decorated longcase with a red ground, like that of the clock shown *above*, produced c.1770 by the London maker Thomas Gardner. As on painted examples, print-decorated longcases always have an arched dial and generally also a pagoda top with gilt finials.
* There are no areas of gesso, or raised work to the trunk, as there are on painted pieces.

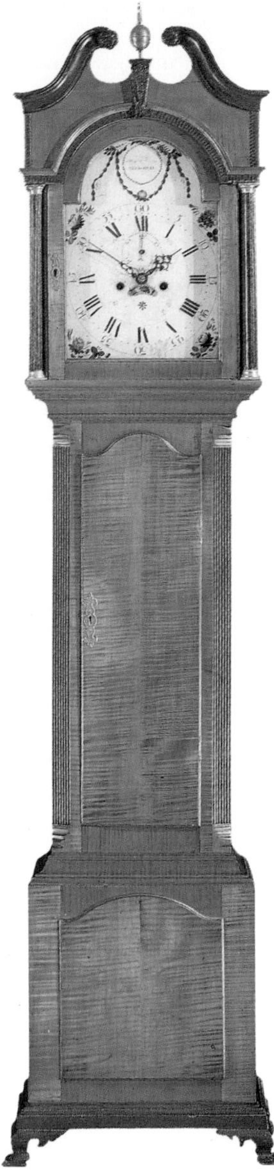

A Federal period tallcase by Luther Goddard; c.1800; ht 87¼in/222cm; value code B

Identification checklist for late 18thC American tallcase clocks
1. Does the case have reeded corners?
2. Has a combination of woods been used? (such as mahogany with maple or cherrywood)
3. Is the top elaborate?
4. Are there any finials? (either brass or wood)
5. Are the hands steel?
6. Does the clock have an arched dial?
7. Does it have bracket feet?
8. Is the clock signed on the dial?

American tallcase clocks
The American longcase, or tallcase clock, first appeared in the late 17thC. Tallcases were made all over the eastern United States, but Pennsylvania, Massachusetts and Connecticut became important centres. The earliest tallcases had square dials, usually of applied brass, with no arch. Cases were plain, especially in the early years. At first, makers followed the English tradition for cases and movements, but by the late 18thC, a uniquely American style had developed.

Movements
Tallcases may be of 30-hour duration, with a brass movement wound by an endless rope (see p.45), or of eight-day duration, with brass movement. A few examples have wooden movements.
* The plates (and occasionally the wheels) of wooden movements can suffer shrinkage and cracking (see p.105).

Cases
Mahogany was very common as a case veneer, but local woods such as cherry or maple were also used, sometimes combined with mahogany. On the clock in the main picture, the case is veneered with maple, and mahogany is used for details such as the base and feet, the

swan's-neck pediment and the freestanding hood columns. Almost all late 18thC American tallcases have an arched top, sometimes with a pagoda and finials or swan's-neck cresting. Elaborate pierced cresting was common, notably the "whale's tails" (see p.43) made by Thomas Harland of Connecticut.
* The trunk may have reeded corners, possibly chamfered or quarter-round, invariably a sign of quality.

Slight variations on the English style became common after the Revolutionary War: the traditional swan's-neck pediment has become notably pronounced on the clock *above*, produced by a New Jersey maker c.1790-1815. Finials vary widely in shape; the fir cone is a fairly common motif. The eagle, a popular American symbol, was also used (and is found on some Edinburgh clocks as well). The mahogany case is inlaid with oval reserves, indicative of quality.
* "French" feet, as on the example shown below left, are very common on American tallcases, as are the "ogee" bracket feet on the clock in the main picture. Both types are subject to damage and loss, either through standing on a damp stone floor or through scraping and bumping.

Value
Early American tallcases are extremely valuable today, but are rarely found outside the United States. No fakes are known.

Dials
As in England, the arched dial is standard for late 18thC American tallcases. However, as on the clock in the main picture, they are predominantly painted metal, rather than brass with applied chapter ring or one-piece engraved and silvered brass.
* The arch may feature painted moons, pastoral or maritime scenes, or even a rocking ship.

The unusual engraved brass dial *above* from a cherrywood tall-case produced c.1800, bears the signature of the prominent maker Eli Terry, of Plymouth Connecticut, who was one of the first Americans to produce clocks in large numbers.
* As on other tallcase clocks, the hands are steel, and are also elaborately pierced.

DUTCH LONGCASES

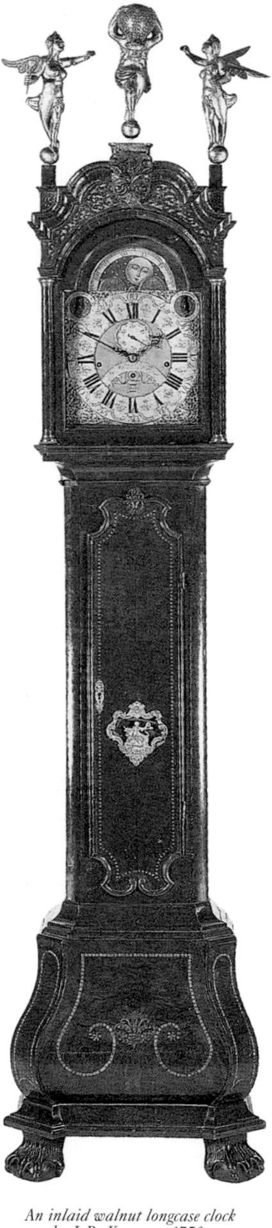

An inlaid walnut longcase clock by J.P. Kroese; c.1750; ht 107½in/273cm; value code C

Identification checklist for 18thC Dutch longcase clocks
1. Is the case walnut-veneered?
2. Does it have a bulbous base section?
3. Does the top have three large figural finials?
4. Are the feet fairly large?
5. Is the dial arched, with applied spandrels and a silvered chapter ring?
6. Is there an ornate surround to the pendulum aperture?
7. Are the hands elaborate?
8. Is the clock signed?

Dutch longcase clocks
Longcase clocks were produced in the Netherlands from the late 17thC, after the Dutch scientist Christian Huyghens (1629-95) fitted a long pendulum to a weight-driven clock. However, they never equalled the quality achieved by English makers. Dutch longcases from the 17thC tend to resemble English ones from the same period, in terms of both cases and movements. Walnut was extensively used as a case veneer. Most 17thC cases have a square dial with a flat-topped hood. With the introduction of larger furniture, such as display cabinets, large and impressive pieces (including clocks) gradually became status symbols for their owners. For this reason, 18thC cases are larger and more elaborate than 17thC examples. However, walnut remained the most common case veneer. They were produced in large numbers, and today are most commonly found in the United States.

The case
One of the most characteristic features of 18thC Dutch longcases is the bulbous, *bombé* base section. The swelling sides of the base sometimes took the form of projecting scrolls. The one-piece trunk door often has a pendulum aperture, similar to the lenticle on English longcases (see p.31), often with an elaborate cast metal surround.

There are some marquetry cases; walnut cases may have decorative stringing or inlay in light-coloured woods.
* Feet are usually substantial, and either paw- or ball-shaped.

The ultimate refinement on 18thC Dutch longcases was the separate stand, or plinth, as on the clock shown *above*, signed "Johannus Petrus Logge" of Amsterdam. As many stands have now been lost, any clock with this feature is a great rarity today.
* The substantial figural finials, showing Atlas with two attendant female figures on either side, are a characteristic feature of 18thC Dutch longcase clocks.

Movements
Movements are of the same basic construction as English longcases. All are weight-driven, usually of eight-day duration, and have an anchor escapement. The long pendulum rod is brass or steel, and has a brass or iron bob. They usually strike the hours on two bells. Many have an alarm.

The dial
Almost all 18thC Dutch longcases have an arched dial, with a silvered chapter ring and applied spandrels (sometimes with flower or harvest motifs). It is common to find indications for both the day of the week and the date. The date aperture, usually triangular in shape, is often very large.
* Dutch longcases are signed on the dial.
* Hands are usually blued steel, and often elaborate.

Dials may have automata or musical work. The rocking figure in the arch of the c.1775 clock *above* is typical.
* Musical work will often require expert overhauling.

Beware
The main drawback of 18thC Dutch longcases is their excessive height. The clock above would have had the standard figural finials. These figures can suffer damage when the clock is moved. Finials may have been removed to fit a clock into a room with a lower ceiling. Missing finials seriously detract from the value of a clock, and are hard to replace.

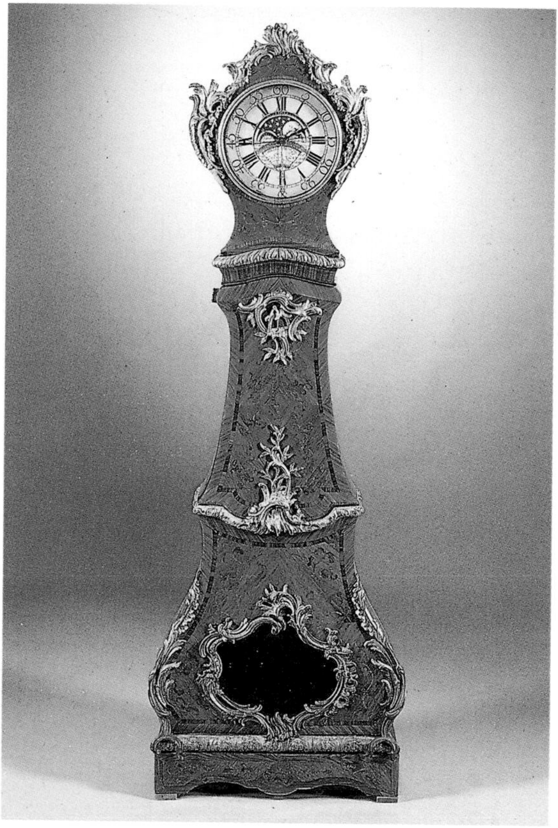

A tulipwood marquetry regulateur *by Louis-François Heurbault c.1750; ht 80½in/204cm; value code A*

Identification checklist for French longcase *regulateurs*
1. Is the top of the case rounded?
2. Does the case swell outward?
3. Is there any applied ormolu decoration?
4. Is the case veneered with marquetry?
5. Does the clock strike the hours?
6. Is there a wide plinth base?
7. Is the dial silvered, with a glass cover and brass bezel?
8. Is there a glazed section to the trunk?

French longcase clocks
Longcase clocks were made in France from the early 18thC. Early examples are highly elaborate, with extensive use of ormolu mounts and marquetry. The best examples, like the *regulateur* in the main picture, were made in Paris. They do not often turn up at auction today.

* *Regulateurs* are weight-driven, with a long pendulum, and often, a pin wheel escapement (see p.10). Most examples strike the hours on a bell.
* Walnut and rosewood are the most common case veneers. Other woods, such as apple, mahogany and tulipwood were used for details of inlay.

Cases
French longcase clocks fall into three styles:
* The *regulateur* has a *bombé* (swelling) trunk.
* The *Comtoise* (see below) has a bulbous centre .
* The *pendule sur socle*, or pedestal clock (see right), is a large bracket clock on a floor-standing pedestal.

Bases
The wide plinth is common on French longcase *regulateurs*. Differences in the colour and figuring of the case veneers often indicate a replaced base.

Additional features
Many French longcases have sophisticated mechanisms or subsidiary dials. The clock in the main picture shows moon phases, seconds, equation and date, and strikes the quarter-hours.

***Comtoise* clocks**
Longcases were made in the French provinces c.1770-1900. They are known as *Comtoise*, because the movements were produced by craftsmen in *Franche-Comté*.
* Most examples strike the hours on a bell (and strike the same hour again two minutes later).

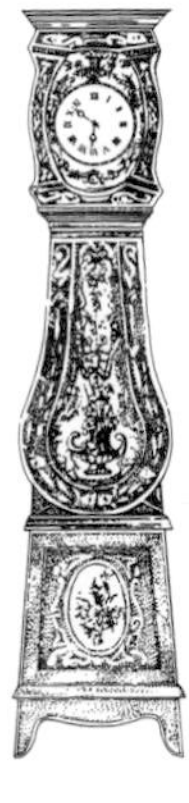

Comtoise clocks often have an elaborate brass pendulum, with a glazed section in the bulbous pine case to allow it to be seen. Early clocks have a cast brass cresting above the convex enamel dial. Late 19thC dials have a cresting of pressed metal.
* Dials are signed by the retailer.
* Cases have often disintegrated due to woodworm and rot. There are few on the market.

Charles-André Boulle
One of the finest French casemakers, the Paris-based Charles-André Boulle (1642-1732), produced extravagant designs of inlaid brass, pewter and tortoiseshell, in a style now known as Boulle marquetry.

Pedestal clocks, like the example with a Boulle case shown *above*, stand on a tapered plinth (often ebonized). The inlay and mounts on the plinth should always match the clock case. Boulle cases usually also have a gilt bronze figure on the top of the clock. Applied enamel dial plaques, as on this example, are common on 18thC French clocks.
* Pedestal clocks are rare. They were made by Paris makers only.
* Because the shape of the case precludes a pendulum, pedestal clocks are spring-driven.

CASE STYLES

The long case was "invented" to contain the weights and the long pendulum hanging below the movement. The case underwent many variations, in terms of shape and woods, from the late 17th to the late 19thC.

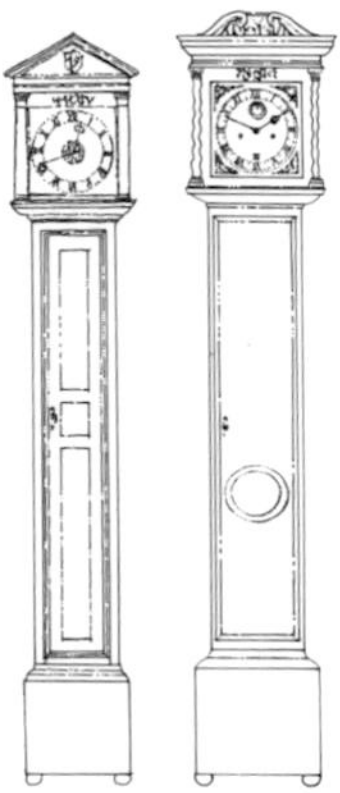

Left Ebony case with architectural top and square dial
c.1665; ht 74in/188cm
Right Walnut case with a lenticle in the trunk door
c.1680; ht 76in/193cm

Left "Arabesque" marquetry case
c.1715; ht 98in/249cm
Right Walnut case (arched dial)
c.1715; ht 108in/274cm

Left Early marquetry case
c.1695; ht 82in/208cm
Right "All-over" marquetry case
c.1700; ht 86in/218cm

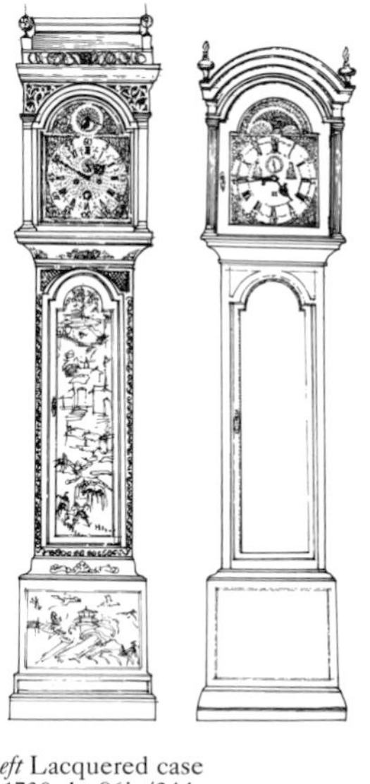

Left Lacquered case
c.1730; ht 96in/244cm
Right Mahogany case (arched top)
c.1750; ht 94in/239cm

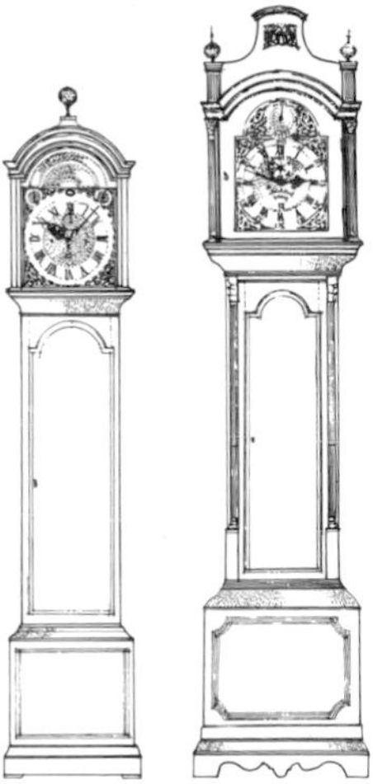

Left Mahogany case by Thomas Mudge with arched top and single finial on a plinth
c.1760; ht 84in/213cm
Right Mahogany case with pagoda top and finials (sound fret in centre of hood top), and shaped, or apron base
c.1770; ht 94in/239cm

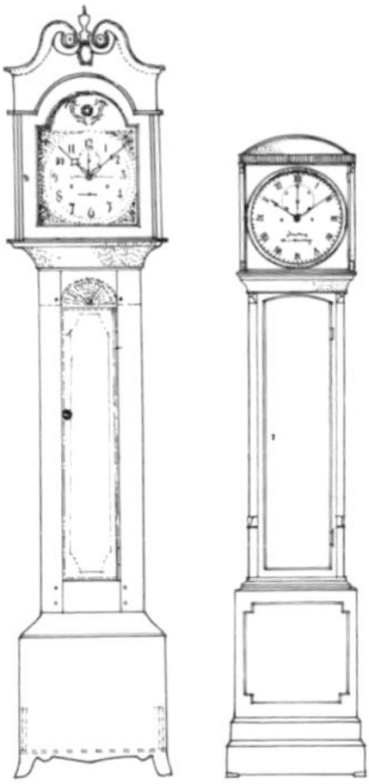

Left American cherrywood case with swan's-neck pediment
c.1800; ht 90in/229cm
Right Mahogany case with rounded top and round dial
c.1815; ht 75½in/192cm

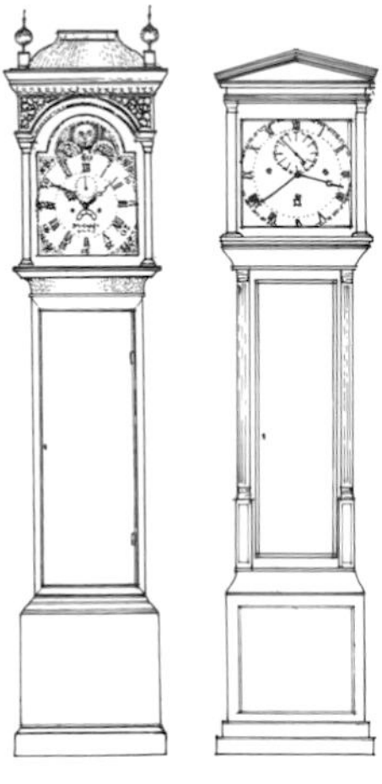

Left Mahogany case (caddy top)
c.1790; ht 88in/223cm
Right Mahogany case
c.1810; ht 84in/213cm

Above Edwardian musical longcase with tubular bells and spectacularly carved case.
c.1905; ht 116in/295cm

Authenticity
Longcase clocks were produced over a long period, with many variations to dial and case. Knowledge of the major stylistic and mechanical developments, and of problem areas peculiar to longcases, can help to distinguish an original piece from one that has been modified.

The parts of the case
The main elements of the long case consist of:
* the hood; encloses the dial and movement. Early longcases had a rising hood. From c.1660-90, the hood was made to slide forward, with a glazed door that opens so that the clock can be wound. Additional features include frets, finials and columns.
* the trunk; the centre section of the case. The trunk door opens to allow adjustment of the long pendulum and fitting of the weights. There may be a window, or *lenticle*, in the middle of the trunk door.
* The base and plinth; the bottom section of the case. The base may be panelled. There may be bun- or pad-shaped feet.

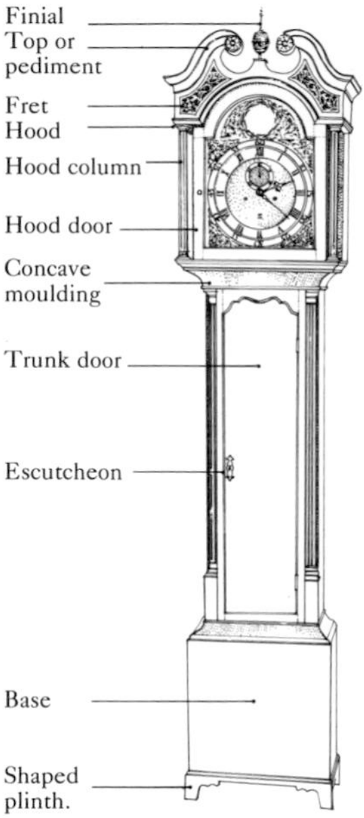

LONGCASE DIALS

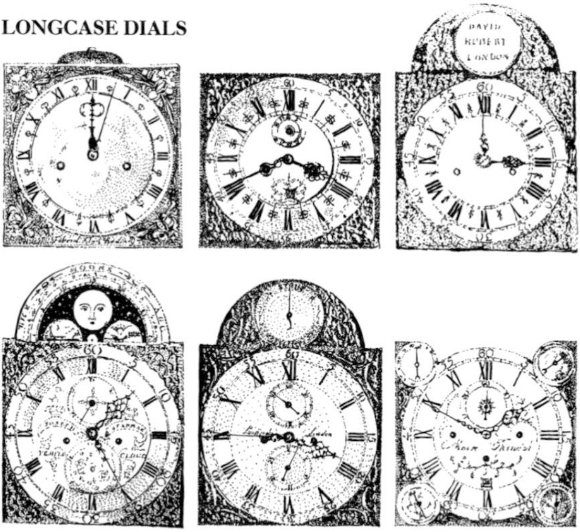

Square dials, *top left*, and *top centre*, were used until c.1715. From c.1715, the arched dial became standard. The arch may be signed by the maker, *top right*; show the phases of the moon, *bottom left*; or have a strike/silent dial, *bottom centre*. Square dials were used in the provinces until the 1840s, *bottom right*.

MARRIAGES

If a movement and dial are not original to the case or to each other, the clock is a "marriage". If case, dial and movement fit together well, a marriage may be acceptable. Ill-fitting ones should be avoided. Marriages occur for several reasons:

* When ebony went out of fashion, the movement and dial from an ebony case were sometimes housed in a walnut or marquetry case.
* When mahogany came into fashion, many arched-dial clocks were taken from walnut cases and put in a mahogany case.
* A dial and/or movement may have been changed to create a false impression of age, and thus boost the clock's value. It is more likely for a movement and dial to be in the wrong case than for a dial and movement to be married. It is acceptable to replace a damaged original dial.

Warning signs

As well as familiarity with the various styles of cases, dials and movements, certain signs help to detect a marriage:

* **Replaced dial:**
* **1.** Four spare holes in the frontplate of the movement, where the original dial was fixed, may indicate a new dial. New feet may have been riveted to the dial plate, and the old holes plugged. The way to discover this is to look at the back of the dial.
* **2.** The dial should fit the hood opening: if a new dial is too large, the masking frame may cover the edges of the chapter ring. The frame itself may have been changed; look for signs of fresh work or new materials, such as plywood.
* **Dial and movement changed**: If the dial and movement have been changed, there may be rubbing marks on the case interior, caused by the weights hanging too far forward, or by a too-large pendulum. Excessive rubbing may mean there is a new movement that is too big for the case. Two sets of marks on the back indicates a replaced pendulum. Look also for pieces cut out of the case interior to allow a larger pendulum swing.
* On cases with a lenticle (see p.31), if the pendulum does not swing opposite the lenticle, then it may be a replacement.
* A month-duration movement is taller than one of eight-day duration. Thus the position of the seatboard – the piece of wood on which the movement sits – will vary if the movement has been changed. Fresh packing pieces may indicate a replaced seatboard.

Fakes

Fakes are less common than marriages. Obvious signs include:

* A fresh-looking case interior
* Very thin veneers (indicates they are machine-cut)
* Re-veneered cases are rare. If the figuring is not appropriate to the style of case or dial, then the veneers may have been changed.

"UPGRADING"

In the late 19thC, some longcase movements were "upgraded", in an attempt to bring them up to date. As well as the normal two trains, a third one may have been added (for the quarter-hours). Wheels and pinions may have been replaced; new wheels have square-edged collets. Upgraded clocks should be avoided.

CASES

Alterations to the case can make a clock look out of proportion. The feet and top are vulnerable:

* A removed cresting may leave a "shadow" or outline on the top. The cresting was fixed by pegs; the peg holes will be visible if the cresting has been removed.
* The case top or feet may have been cut to reduce the height of the clock.
* The base may have been cut, if damaged by woodworm (see below) or rot. A new base may be different in shape or grain.
* Oak and pine cases are easily affected by woodworm. Small dry holes indicate woodworm. In most cases the worm is inactive; fine white powder in the holes and on the floor nearby indicates it is active. Active woodworm, which is rare, must be treated; if extensive, the clock should be avoided.

HANDS

It is preferable to have original hands, but good replacements are acceptable (see p.15).

The winding key

A replaced key is acceptable, as the original (appears pitted and aged) has usually been lost.

BRACKET CLOCKS

A walnut bracket clock by John Wady, c.1720

Today, "bracket" remains the umbrella description for spring-driven clocks with a short pendulum designed to stand on a surface, such as a table, shelf or wall bracket, although originally, only a few "bracket clocks" were ever displayed on a separate wall bracket. They are sometimes referred to as "table" clocks. However, this term really describes only some early examples. The clockmakers themselves often preferred to describe bracket clocks as "spring" clocks, as all examples are driven by a coiled steel spring rather than hanging weights. "Mantel clock" is also an acceptable term, but usually refers to relatively small clocks produced during the first half of the 19thC. In the United States, where they were produced in large numbers, bracket clocks are commonly known as "shelf clocks".

Bracket clocks were developed from c.1660, or roughly the same time as longcase clocks. Many makers of longcases probably also made bracket clocks (and usually watches as well). However, production was always much more confined to London than was the case with longcases: there are few notable English provincial bracket makers. Developments in the style, shape and size of both case and dial largely followed the longcase pattern. Woods used include ebony, walnut, mahogany and rosewood. Some cases also feature lacquer decoration or complex applied metalwork.

Early brackets have a square brass dial, typically with an applied chapter ring. The arched dial became increasingly common from c.1715. Silvered brass dials were used from c.1760 and painted metal dials from c.1780. The round dial – sometimes enamelled – is a feature of brackets from the late 18thC and the Regency period.

Originally, all bracket clocks had a verge escapement (see p.10). The verge was a more robust mechanism than the anchor escapement (see p.10), but was considerably less accurate. It also required a less precise and less stable setting than did the anchor. In the 19thC, many clocks with verge escapements were converted to anchor. In some cases, this was done elegantly, but there are many crude conversions. The quality of the conversion will be a major factor in the value of a clock. It is often worthwhile to reconvert to a verge escapement if a clock is particularly important or valuable.

All bracket clocks are spring-driven. Most strike the hours (and sometimes also the quarter-hours). The steel spring which powers the clock is coiled in a barrel. As it unwinds, the force of the spring lessens. To maintain an even supply of power, bracket clocks incorporate a conical gearing device known as a fusee (see p.11).

In the 1840s, the advent of the American bracket, or shelf clock, with its mass-produced, stamped components, led to the gradual decline of the English bracket clock. Mass production meant that the American clocks were considerably less expensive than English ones. Bracket clocks from the Continent of Europe, mainly France, enjoyed considerable popularity in England, particularly during the 19thC, but never on the same scale as carriage clocks (see pp.130-43). Both American and European clocks are popular today, and French bracket clocks in particular represent good value for money.

The most collectable English bracket clocks on the market are mahogany-veneered examples – with either bell or arched top – produced during the second half of the 18thC, and mahogany and rosewood cases from the Regency period. Both types are still available in substantial numbers. The Regency clocks may be a good investment, as they have never been quite as sought-after as 18thC mahogany cases, and thus their prices are still comparatively low.

Unlike longcase clocks, it is extremely unlikely that a bracket dial or movement will have been changed, or married, to a different case. Bracket movements are always securely fixed to the case. By contrast, longcase movements can simply be lifted out of the case. Bracket clocks have only rarely been faked, although some have been recased.

WALNUT AND OLIVE BRACKETS

A walnut bracket clock with an arched dial by John Ellicott c.1760; ht 19in/48cm; value code A

Identification checklist for early bracket clocks, c.1670-1710 (excluding ebony – see pp.64-5)
1. Is the clock veneered with walnut? (or, in some cases, olivewood)
2. Are all the mouldings cross-grained?
3. Is the back of the case veneered (as well as the front and sides)?
4. Do the veneers show the signs of age, such as slight lifting at the edges?
5. Does the clock have a striking mechanism?
6. Does it have a brass carrying handle?
7. Does the case have a cushion top?
8. Is there a five-minute ring on the dial?
9. Does the clock have a signature on the backplate as well as on the dial?
10. Are the hands blued steel?

Early walnut bracket clocks
Bracket clocks, or clocks designed to stand on a wall bracket, a table or a shelf, appeared from c.1670. The earliest examples have walnut or olivewood cases. They are all of eight-day duration, and most strike the hours. Early examples have a square brass dial. Arched dials came into use from c.1725. Almost all square-dial clocks were by London makers, but arched-dials were also produced by provincial makers.

Cases
Early bracket clocks are veneered on the back, sides and front. Mouldings vary in shape, especially on the base, but should be cross-grained (at right angles to the main veneer). Most have a brass carrying handle. Feet may be pad or bun, but are often damaged or replaced.

Sides may be glazed, as on the rare 11in/29cm-high miniature *above*, by Henry Jones, c.1680, or have glass or wooden frets (although many wooden frets have been replaced by glass). Any 17th or 18thC glass is very desirable; it is thinner than modern glass, with a rippled surface and tiny air bubbles.
* "Cushion" tops are typical of early brackets.
* The dials on early bracket clocks always have engraved spandrels. (Applied spandrels are standard on later versions.)
* Early brackets can be dated by their narrow five-minute ring, as this became considerably wider during the 18thC.

Movements
Early English bracket clocks are all spring-driven, with fusee movement (see p.11). All early examples originally had a verge escapement, but many were later converted to anchor escapement in order to improve their accuracy. Some were later converted back to verge.

The short pendulum with bulbous bob, as shown *above*, is typical of a verge escapement. If converted to anchor, the apron at the top of the rod would have been removed. If reconverted to verge, a new one would have been added, perhaps in a different style.
* The backplate is signed by the maker, Henry Jones. Most early bracket clocks are signed on both backplate and dial.

The olivewood "oyster" veneer on the clock *above*, made by William Knottesford c.1685, was used only on the very finest quality bracket clocks. "Oyster" cases are very rare, but the twist columns are a characteristic feature of clocks in this wood.

An ebony-veneered bracket clock by John Gwilt c.1695, ht 15½in/39cm; value code A

Identification checklist for ebony-veneered and ebonized bracket clocks

1. If the case is ebonized (stained black), is it slightly worn, with no signs of re-ebonizing?
2. Are there any complex metal mounts or escutcheons?
3. Does the clock have brass bun feet?
4. Is the movement secured to the case with brackets or screws in the original positions? (indicating that it is original to the case)
5. If there is an apron to the back cock, does it match the rest of the backplate? (see opposite)
6. Is the clock striking? (i.e., with two winding holes)
7. Does it have quarter-repeating work?
8. Are the hands blued steel, with an elaborate hour hand and a simple minute hand?
9. Is the piece signed on the backplate and on (or very rarely, above) the dial?

Ebony-veneered and ebonized bracket clocks

Bracket clocks with ebony veneer are contemporary with walnut and olive cases (see pp.62-3), and began to appear c.1670. Ebonized cases were common from c.1705. Ebony or ebonized pieces average 15in/38cm in height. Early examples have a square dial, with arched dials more common on later ones. They were made in London.

Woods

Ebonized brackets generally use pale fruitwood veneer, typically apple or pear wood, stained black. Veneers are applied to the back and sides as well as to the front. If worn, the pale-coloured fruitwood shows through.

Typical features

Ebony-veneered and ebonized brackets typically include:
* a brass carrying handle
* brass side frets and case mounts
* a brass dial with applied chapter ring and spandrels.

Complex metal mounts and escutcheons are common on early bracket clocks. The "pierced basket" top, brass side frets and *repoussé* brass mounts on the ebony-veneered clock *above*, made by John Shaw c.1685, indicate a piece of the highest quality.

Signatures

The backplate and the dial are usually signed. It is unusual for the signature to appear above the dial, as it does on the clock in the main picture, or below it.

Movements

Movements are basically the same as for walnut brackets. Nearly all clocks are striking, and typically repeat the quarter-hours on two or three bells when a repeat cord is pulled. All examples originally had verge escapements. However, like walnut bracket clocks, many were later converted to anchor escapement (and possibly back again to verge; see p.63). If the brackets or screws which secure the movement to the case seem to be in their original position, this indicates that the movement is probably original.
* Later ebonized brackets may have an original anchor escapement.
* The screen over the top of the pendulum rod, known as the apron to the back cock, will have been removed if the clock has been converted.

On this arched-dial bracket clock, *above*, made by Justin Vulliamy c.1750, the ebonized surface has worn in places, exposing the pale-coloured veneer underneath. This piece has the "inverted bell" top typical of 18thC clocks. The mock pendulum aperture in the upper part of the centre is connected to the escapement, and shows that the clock is ticking.
* Worn ebonizing may have been reblacked. Hastily executed work can detract from a clock's value.

A mahogany bracket clock with a bell top by Benjamin Ward c.1785; ht 20in/51cm; value code D

Identification checklist for mahogany bracket clocks
1. Does the clock have an arched dial?
2. Are the veneers of good colouring and figuring?
3. If a bell top case, are finials pineapple or urn-shaped?
4. Is the back door glazed? (rather than veneered)
5. Is there a door to both the back and front of the case?
6. Does the case have brass bracket feet?
7. Does the clock have an hour-repeat mechanism?
8. Is the clock signed on the dial?
9. Are the hands blued steel?
10. Does it have a strike/silent lever (see p.12)?

Mahogany bracket clocks
Generally larger than walnut or ebony brackets, mahogany bracket clocks stand around 20in/51cm in height. Mahogany was used for cases from c.1730 until the 1830s.

Movements
Originally, most mahogany brackets had a verge escapement (see p.10). However, some of these clocks will have been converted to anchor. (For signs of conversion, see p.63.)

The case

Cases vary considerably, and some are extremely elaborate. Backs are almost always glazed. Side frets may be glazed or of pierced brass. The bell top is typical of early mahogany brackets, but arched tops became common from c.1785. Some tops have mahogany pads edged with brass mouldings.

* Finials are often missing or have been replaced by those of a later period or different style.
* The dial is almost always signed. It is uncommon for a mahogany piece to be signed on the backplate as well.

The opulent bracket clock *above*, produced by Eardley Norton c.1780, has three trains, one of which automatically strikes the quarter-hours. In addition to striking the hours, most mahogany brackets also have hour-repeating work – which repeats the last hour struck when a cord attached to the movement is pulled. The cord and lever have sometimes been removed. Repeating work is a desirable feature with this type of clock.

* The paw feet and brass base on this clock are unusually elaborate, but contribute to the decorative feel of the clock.
* Original brass finials should all be of matching design and patina. If they do not match, some of the set may not be original. If the finials do match but there are signs of disturbance to the case top, the whole set may be replacements.

The round silvered dial on the clock *above* – with original wall bracket – is unusual for a mahogany bracket clock, as are the pad feet. It was produced by Richard Webster c.1790. Because it is a late piece, it has an original anchor escapement (see p.63).

* Any clock with an original wall bracket is highly desirable.

An alternative to mahogany was satinwood, which became popular towards the end of the 18thC. Balloon bracket clocks, like the example shown *above*, made by William Addis c.1780, often have satinwood-veneered cases. This style of case also appeared in ebonized wood, but is not common in mahogany.

LACQUERED BRACKETS

A bracket clock with a lacquered case by Stephen Rimbault, c.1775; ht 18¾in/47cm; value code C

Identification checklist for lacquered-case bracket clocks
1. Does the clock have a bell top? (or an inverted bell top)
2. Is the base shaped rather than simply flat?
3. Is the case decorated with Chinoiserie motifs?
4. Are there any wood frets fitted to the sides and doors?
5. Are the finials a complete set?
6. Is there any raised gesso on the front of the case?
7. Does the arched dial have an applied chapter ring and spandrels?
8. Is the clock signed?
9. Are the hands blued steel?

Lacquered bracket clocks
Bracket clocks with lacquered cases are much rarer today than lacquered longcases. Roughly comparable in size to mahogany bracket clocks (see pp.66-7), they were produced during the mid-18thC, mainly by London makers. Chinoiserie motifs cover the sides and back, as well as the

front of the case. The best examples have the same quality of decoration on both back and front. The bell shape is the most common top.

Movements
Movements are identical to those of mahogany brackets. Lacquered cases most commonly have a verge escapement (see p.10), strike the hours on a bell, and repeat the last hour struck when a cord connected to the movement is pulled.

Unusually, this very early black-ground clock, *above*, produced by James Boyce c.1705, has a square brass dial. Lacquered brackets usually have an arched dial. Both square and arched dials invariably feature an applied brass chapter ring and applied spandrels. Typically, there are few other metal mounts, apart from finials and carrying handle. This clock has side handles, instead of the usual characteristic carrying handle on the top of the case, and has a cushion top instead of a bell top.
* Hands are always blued steel, and, as on this example, may be elaborately pierced.

Signatures
All examples are signed. The signature is usually on the dial or in the arch, but not on the backplate. Instead, the backplate typically features engraved decoration; either scrolling or Chinoiserie. On the clock in the main picture, the signature is on a plaque in the dial centre.

Lacquerwork
Red was the most popular ground colour. However, as with lacquered longcase clocks (see pp.46-9), black or green is common. Green grounds often become black with age.
* The lacquerwork should be as original and as untouched as possible. Some fading is desirable, as it is a sign of age, and is therefore preferable to over-restored lacquer. If the lacquer appears very bright, this may indicate that restoration has been carried out.
* Original lacquer decoration is subject to lifting or flaking (For condition of lacquered cases, see p.47).

By c.1765, wooden frets had been replaced by glass sides, like those of the clock by William Clarke shown *above*. As on mahogany brackets, the back panel is glazed. The glazed areas flanking the dial arch on the clock in the main picture may be original features rather than later replacements, designed to reveal the lacquer decoration behind the door, which matches that on the rest of the case.
* Finials on lacquered bracket clocks may be missing or replaced. Look for a matching set, with no signs of disturbance to the case top. The finials on this piece are unusual: the pineapple form is more common.
* The shaped bottom is common on lacquered-case brackets.

A rosewood chamfer-top bracket clock by M. Gilkes c.1820; ht 20½in/52cm; value code E

Identification checklist for chamfer-top bracket clocks

1. Does the case have a steep chamfer top with a pineapple finial, or a shallow chamfer without a finial?
2. Is the case rosewood or mahogany?
3. Is there brass inlay to the front of the case?
4. Does the case have brass ball feet? (wood feet are rare)
5. Are there any brass frets?
6. Are there any ring handles on the sides?
7. Does the clock have a round convex dial?
8. Does the clock strike the hours?
9. Does it have an anchor escapement?
10. Is the clock signed on the dial?
11. Are the hands simple brass or blued steel?

Regency bracket clocks
After the well-defined styles of the 18thC, bracket clocks from the Regency period (1811-20) show a great diversity in both case and dial, although the case is generally mahogany or rosewood (sometimes ebonized).
* All clocks have glazed backs. Unless there are brass frets on the sides of the case, these will also be glazed.

Chamfer-top brackets
Of the bracket clocks produced around the Regency period, those with a chamfer top are among the most distinctive. Like the clock in the main picture, most were made by London makers. The chamfer top may be steep or fairly shallow. The sides usually have original brass "fish-scale" frets with silk backing. These tend to have survived because brass frets are stronger than the wood used on earlier clocks. Chamfer-top brackets have a round dial; because this is always convex, the glass covering the dial is also convex, and is surrounded by a hinged brass bezel locked from the side.
* The brass ball feet on all the clocks shown here are a typical Regency feature. Alternatively, there may be shallow wooden pad feet, but these are rare.
* Some pieces originally had a wall bracket. Today, these are likely to be replacements. Measurements refer to the clock only, without the bracket.

Movements
Almost all chamfer-top brackets were originally fitted with an anchor escapement, and there are few conversions from verge. All are of eight-day duration, strike the hours on a bell, and have a fusee movement (see p.11). When pulled, the repeat cord, like that at the side of the clock shown on p.74, repeats the last hour struck. There is typically a strike/silent lever (see p.12) at the top of the dial.

Hands
The hands of Regency brackets are simpler than those of earlier bracket clocks, and are either brass or blued steel. Usually there is a spade-tipped hour hand and a plain minute hand, or else pierced-tip hands with some elaboration, as on the clock in the main picture.

Scrolling or floral brass inlay, sometimes fairly intricate in design – as on the ebonized clock *above*, produced by Hanson of Windsor c.1805 – is a characteristic feature of chamfer-top bracket clocks. The ribs on this shallow top supply a Neo-classical touch. The corners of the case are also chamfered, and strung with brass.
* Inlaid brass decoration usually appears only on the front and sides of the case.

The dial may be engraved and silvered brass, painted iron or, as on the clock *above*, made by Barrauds c.1820, fired enamel on copper. Dials are always signed.
* Side handles are common on pieces with a chamfer top. These clocks have a pineapple finial, and no top handle. Shallow tops, like this, may be plain.

REGENCY BRACKETS: 2

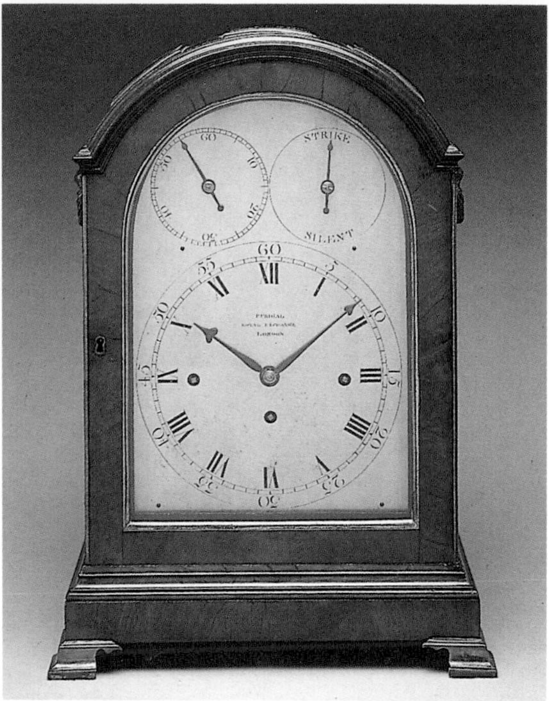

A mahogany quarter-striking bracket clock by Francis Perigal c.1800; ht 18in/46cm; value code D

Identification checklist for Regency and early 19thC bracket clocks (apart from chamfer tops – see pp.70-1)
1. Is the case highly decorative? (possibly with an arched or rounded top)
2. If a veneered case, is it mahogany? (some are rosewood)
3. Are the sides glazed?
4. Is the back of the case glazed?
5. Is the clock spring-driven?
6. Does it have a signature on the dial? (and perhaps on the movement)
7. Are the hands made of blued steel?

Other Regency and early 19thC bracket clocks
The first half of the 19thC, and particularly the Regency period (1811-20), saw a great diversity of bracket styles, in addition to the chamfer top (see pp.70-1). Examples from this period vary widely in the size and shape of the case. Like most English bracket clocks – and unlike longcases – they were made in London. Some examples by provincial makers can be found (usually with London-made movements).

Cases
Like the clock in the main picture, cases are usually mahogany-veneered, although quite a few are of rosewood or ebonized wood. Many have a plain arched top, typically with brass-edged wooden pads on top of the case. Three pads, as on the clock in the main picture, is a sign of quality.
* Like the example in the main picture, many pieces have no carrying handle.

Feet may be ball- or bracket-shaped: bracket feet, as on the c.1815 clock *above*, produced by John Heywood, are more typical of turn-of-the-century examples.
* The back is glazed. Unless there are brass "fish-scale" frets, as on the clock above, the sides are also glazed.

Value
Early 19thC brackets are still available in large numbers. Regency pieces may be a good investment, as they have not been as sought-after as 18thC mahogany cases.

Movements
Early 19thC examples are spring-driven, with a fusee movement and usually with an anchor escapement, although some have a verge (see p.10). Most are of eight-day duration. Like the Heywood clock above, most early 19thC clocks strike the hours.

Dials
Round dials became common in the 19thC, but the dials of early 19thC clocks show a great deal of variation. They may be round or arched. The full-width arch, as on the clock in the main picture, is a 19thC feature.

The dial may be engraved and silvered brass, or else painted, enamelled or gilded metal. The convex enamel dial, as on the c.1810 timepiece with top finial *above*, became increasingly common in the early 19thC. The maker's signature usually appears on the dial, and sometimes also on the backplate of the movement. Both the dial and the movement of this example are signed by the maker, John Grant of Fleet Street.

With its black marble base, applied mouldings and engine-turned gilded dial, this small drum timepiece, *above*, made by William Webster c.1850, shows a French influence (see p.82-3).
* Hands are usually blued steel, and often have heart, spade or moon motifs (open or pierced). The pierced heart-tipped hands on the clock above are typical.

FOUR-GLASS BRACKETS

A rosewood four-glass bracket clock by Lister of Newcastle c.1840, ht 11in/28cm; value code C/D

Identification checklist for four-glass bracket clocks
1. Does the case have a flat top?
2. Is there a projecting moulding around the top?
3. Does the brass handle have a straight centre section, with elaborately shaped ends?
4. Are there any brass bun feet?
5. Does the clock strike on a gong?
6. Is it signed?
7. Are the hands blued steel?

Four-glass bracket clocks
Four-glass bracket (or mantel) clocks, made between c.1815 and 1845, take their name from the glazed areas on the front, sides, back and top. They are basically rectangular, with a flat top, and are usually 10-11in/25-28cm in height. The most typical feature of four-glass clocks is the carrying handle (although a few were made without it). The handle may be folded flat. It nearly always has a straight centre section and elaborately shaped ends. Four-glass brackets are a London phenomenon.
* In spite of the carrying handle, few four-glass bracket clocks were made with travelling cases.

Signatures
Examples are always signed, usually on the dial and sometimes on the backplate. Although the piece in the main picture bears the signature of a Newcastle retailer, it is likely to have been made in London. The best makers of this type of clock included Edward Dent, Charles Viner and William Frodsham.

Condition
Because most pieces were produced relatively late in comparison with other types of clock, they have not undergone as much wear. In addition, four-glass pieces were expensive, so owners treated them with care and did not sell them. For this reason, they are rare today, with few examples on the market.

Rosewood and satinwood are the most common case veneers, although some clocks, like the one shown *above*, made by Kleyser of Southwark c.1840, have a mahogany case. The top moulding is typical of this type of clock. The base always has a moulded section as well. The flat top may include a bevelled glass section.

Movements
Most four-glass brackets strike the hours on a coiled wire gong, but there are many timepieces. All have a fusee movement (see p.11). Many have an anchor escapement, but the best have a platform lever escapement (see p.10). Like the example in the main picture, these are wound from the back.

* The pull-cord at the right of the clock in the main picture repeats the last hour struck.
* The loud/soft lever, like that on the left of the clock in the main picture, is a desirable refinement. When moved up or down, it activates a two-headed hammer, striking a gong with hardwood (for loud) or leather (for soft).

Dials
The dial may be either silvered with engraved numbers, or, like the piece in the main picture, engraved all over and gilded. The latter type is more valuable.

The metal surround to the dial, known as the sight ring, may be gilded or, as on this satinwood piece, *above*, produced by W. Johnson c.1830, silvered.
* Any spandrels are engraved.
* Brass bun feet are typical.
* Hands are nearly always made of blued steel, and are usually fairly simple in shape.

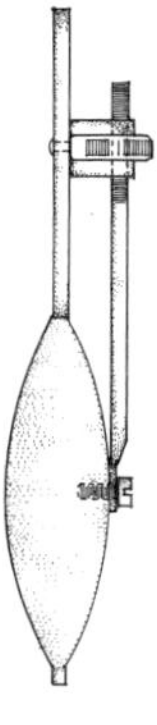

Authenticity
Because they are so small, many four-glass clocks with an anchor escapement have a rating nut (*left*) above, rather than under the bob. This "inverted rating mechanism" consists of a threaded rod, linked by a bracket to the pendulum rod, and connected to the bob. A clock with this feature is likely to have an original anchor.

A bracket clock with a Boulle-style inlaid case by Jacques Maire c.1700; ht 20in/51cm; value code C

Identification checklist for Viennese bracket clocks
1. Is the case elaborate? (with exotic woods, inlay or mounts)
2. Is the dial arched, with an applied chapter ring? (early 18thC), or else enamelled (late 18th and early 19thC)
3. Are the sides glazed?
4. Does the clock have any additional features, either in the striking mechanism or on the dial?
5. Is there a verge escapement? (i.e. a short pendulum)
6. Is the hour hand more ornate than the minute hand?
7. Is the clock signed?

Viennese bracket clocks
Bracket clocks were produced by Viennese makers from c.1700 until c.1820. They were made in small numbers, with the majority intended for sale within the Austrian empire. A few may have been exported to France. A group of Genevan clockmakers settled in Vienna in the late

18thC, and many clocks from this time show the influence of French, German and Swiss styles. As well as Vienna, there were makers in Prague, Budapest and other cities of the empire.

Value point
There are very few Viennese bracket clocks in circulation outside Austria. They are not necessarily expensive to acquire, but many are of two-day duration, which, for some collectors, limits their appeal.

Dials
The dial is usually brass, with an applied silvered chapter ring. From the late 18thC, enamel dials are common. Early 18thC dials may be square, but most dials are arched, and simple in appearance. However, the clock in the main picture has subsidiary dials for date, day, month, moon phase and strike/silent.

Movements
Viennese bracket clocks usually have a verge escapement, with a short pendulum (see p.10). Unlike English brackets, few have been converted to anchor escapement. Elaborate striking mechanisms are common: the clock in the main picture strikes the hours and quarter-hours on six bells. Most examples have a going barrel, but some have a fusee movement (see p.11).

On the early 18thC clock *above*, made by Ferdinant Muller, the pendulum hangs in front of the dial. This feature is found only on Austrian and Black Forest clocks (see p.104).
* Viennese brackets may run for as little as one day.

The three train clock *above*, made by Anton Rettich c.1810, has *grande sonnerie* striking on two bells. The enamelled dial is more typical of late 18th French clocks.

Cases
Cases are generally ornate, and may feature exotic wood veneers, metal mounts or, as on the clock in the main picture, complex brass and pewter inlay.

The late 18thC clock *above*, made by Peter Lazarus, is veneered with coromandel, a wood rarely used by clockmakers.
* Sides tend to be glazed.
* Backplates may be engraved.
* Brass feet are common.
* Many examples have brass top finials, but these are often lost.
* The signature is usually on the backplate rather than on the dial.

EARLY 18THC FRENCH BRACKETS

A Louis XIV tortoiseshell-veneered bracket clock by Claude Artus c.1690; ht 24in/61cm; value code D/E

Identification checklist for 17th and early 18thC French bracket clocks
1. Is the clock striking, on a bell?
2. Is the case elaborate?
3. Does the clock have a going barrel rather than a fusee movement? (see p.11)
4. If brass, are the hands elaborate?
5. Is there any applied metal decoration?
6. Is the piece signed on the dial, and possibly also on the backplate?

Early 18thC French bracket clocks
Encouraged by royal and aristocratic patronage, the production of bracket clocks flourished in France during the 17th and early 18thC, although the greatest profusion of styles is found during the 19thC. Because clocks were seen as decorative

objects, French bracket clocks have far more ornate cases than their English counterparts of the period. Most pieces were produced by Paris makers. Early French bracket clocks are fairly rare today.

Typical features
The clock in the main picture – a *pendule religieuse* – has many of the features typical of early 18thC French brackets, including:
* inlaid and applied metal decoration, such as the gilded bronze lambrequin (ornamental hanging) on the edge of the plinth
* exotic veneers, in this case tortoiseshell
* a detachable base.

The dial
The chapter ring of early French brackets often consists of separate enamel plaques (cartouches), as on the piece in the main picture, on a velvet ground. Velvet was used only on early French and some Dutch brackets. Because it suffers wear and damage from moths, it has often been replaced.

Dials varied widely throughout the 17th and early 18thC, but by the mid-18thC the one-piece enamel or porcelain dial – either convex or flat – had become widespread. As on the striking clock with convex enamel dial shown *below left* – produced by Voisin c.1750 – the elaborate, asymmetrical cast ormolu (gilded or gold-coloured metal) case is typical of the extravagant Rococo style, which flourished under the Regency (1715-23), and during the reign of Louis XV.
* On clocks with an enamel or porcelain dial, a hinged circular glass bezel covers the dial.
* The example shown above does not have a separate base, but others would have stood on a detachable plinth.

Movements
Early French brackets are nearly always striking clocks with verge escapement, but with a going barrel rather than a fusee movement (see p.11). Most strike the hours on a bell, and may also strike the half-hours.

On the very early ebony-veneered bracket clock *above*, made by Menu c.1675, the single winding hole also operates the striking mechanism in addition to the going train. Unlike the clock in the main picture, this example would not have stood on a plinth.
* Hands may be brass or blued steel. Brass hands can be quite elaborate, as on the piece above. Blued steel hands tend to be more severe in appearance.

Signatures
On enamel and porcelain dials, the signature usually appears on the dial. The signature may also be engraved on the backplate.

LATE 18THC FRENCH BRACKETS

A gilt and marble lyre clock by Bisson c.1795; ht 24in/61cm; value code D

Identification checklist for late 18thC French brackets
1. Is the form of the clock elaborate?
2. Is the dial round, with a decorated brass surround?
3. Does the clock have a marble base?
4. Does it feature any applied gilt ornament?
5. Are the hands relatively elaborate?
6. Is the clock signed on the dial?

Late 18thC French bracket clocks
French bracket clocks from the late 18thC show an astonishing variety of styles and decoration. This stylistic diversity, marked by elegant Neo-classical influences, followed the exuberance of early 18thC Rococo. By the late 18thC,

common case styles included the portico and other architectural forms, and figure groups. The lyre, as on the clock in the main picture, was a very popular design. French clocks from this period were made primarily in Paris. They are reasonably common outside France today.

Movements

Most pieces have an anchor escapement, and strike the hours on a bell. Some have a pin wheel escapement (see p.10). Visible movements are rare, except on lyre clocks. On the clock in the main picture, the movement and dial form the bob of the gridiron pendulum (see p.11).

Hands

Hands are typically elaborate, and are often brass. Many pieces also have a slim steel date hand with a counterpoise. Because the date hand was often very long, it had to be strong, and so was often made of steel.

The dial

The vast majority of late 18thC French brackets have a round, convex dial, either porcelain or enamelled. Numbers are usually fired under the glaze.

* The dial surround is usually decorated brass, and may feature engine-turning or a cast pattern.

This small gilt metal *pendule d'officier* with enamel dial, *above*, produced by Meuron c.1795 and only 9in/23cm in height, might have been carried on campaign. Like this example, many French bracket clocks from this period have Arabic numerals.

* On most late 18thC clocks, the back is glazed or solid brass, and either hinged or of lift-out type.

Cases

The cases of late 18thC French bracket clocks are commonly either marble or cast bronze, and make extensive use of applied bronze and gilded metal ornament. Where wood is used, mahogany is the most common.

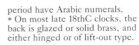

The Revolutionary clock, *above*, made by Duval c.1795, has decimal hours and applied ormolu decoration.

Animal and African figures are common, as on this bronze and gilt bronze *Directoire* mantel clock, *above*, produced by Ridel of Paris c.1800. The choice of animals varies; a tortoise, as here, is uncommon.

* Bronze cases are usually in very good condition, as bronze does not suffer wear or deterioration.

An ormolu and marble clock, from a garniture by Léchopié c.1800; ht 19in/48cm; value code E

Identification checklist for 19thC French bracket clocks
1. Is the form relatively unusual?
2. Does the clock have an anchor escapement?
3. Does it strike on a bell?
4. Is the case metal?
5. Is the clock decorative, possibly featuring ormolu mounts, elaborate hands or figural work?
6. Does it have a round dial?
7. Does the clock have a maker's signature, or possibly a stamped mark on the movement?

19thC French bracket clocks
The 18thC proliferation of styles and shapes of French bracket clocks continued throughout the 19thC. Like their 18thC predecessors, these pieces were not mass-produced but were crafted by small makers based in Paris. Large numbers of French clocks were exported during the 19thC. The ormolu and marble clock shown in the main picture, part of a garniture which includes a matching pair of candelabra (not shown), is in a highly decorative style which became very popular in the late 19thC, particularly in England. Most 19thC French brackets average 20in/51cm in height.

Signatures
The signature may be on both the dial and movement. Mass production of movements began late in the century, so pieces from this period may feature a serial number and maker's mark stamped on the movement.

Typical features
Although there is great variety, features common to 19thC French brackets include:
* a round dial, either porcelain or enamelled
* a marble base
* brass figures
* applied brass, or ormolu, decoration
* blued steel hands. The elaborate brass hands on the clock in the main picture show that it was probably made around the turn of the century.

Movements
A growing interest in precision at this time meant that even decorative clocks are accurate timekeepers. Almost all examples are of eight-day duration, with an anchor escapement.

One-piece porcelain dials are most common, but some dials are two-piece, as on the c.1870 bronze and enamel clock shown *above*, with an enamelled centre and a gilt chapter ring.
* Backs may be glazed or metal, and either hinged or lift-out.

The portico clock, like the gilt bronze example *above*, produced by Armingaud c.1815, was a popular early 19thC style. The gridiron pendulum on this clock compensates for changes in temperature (see p.11).

The French four-glass clock – so-called because of its four glass panes – became common from c.1850. These pieces are usually rectangular, although the example shown *above*, produced c.1870 with a two-piece enamel dial, is oval. The pendulum, made of two mercury-filled glass cylinders, is typical. Cases are polished or gilded brass.
* A few four-glass clocks from this period have wooden cases.

A "wagon-spring" shelf clock by Birge and Fuller c.1850; ht 26in/66cm; value code E

Identification checklist for American shelf clocks
1. Does the case have an unusual shape?
2. Is it veneered with mahogany? (over a pine carcass)
3. Is the back of the case solid, with access to the movement from the front?
4. Does the clock feature a panel of *verre eglomisé* (reverse-painted glass)?
5. Is the dial of painted metal or wood?
6. Does the clock strike the hours on a gong?
7. Does it have the maker's name stamped anywhere on the movement?
8. Is there a label pasted to the back of the case interior bearing the maker's name?

American shelf clocks
American shelf, or bracket clocks differ greatly in appearance and in movements from English bracket clocks of the same period. They were first produced c.1800 and in the United States represented the first application of mass production to clock-making. The Connecticut maker

Chauncey Jerome began to mass-produce movements in 1836-37. By 1845, the Connecticut clock industry was turning out one million shelf clocks annually. Huge numbers were exported to Britain and Europe.

Cases
The cases of American shelf clocks vary considerably in shape. The "steeple" shape on the clock in the main picture is a common style. Variations include the "round Gothic" case, with a rounded top and a round dial. Most shelf clocks are mahogany-veneered, over a pine carcass. Backs are solid wood: the clock front must be opened in order to gain access to the movement. There are no side doors.

The "acorn" clock, *above*, made c.1835 by J.C. Brown, has a panel of *verre eglomisé* (reverse-painted glass): a classic feature of American shelf and wall clocks (see pp.102-3). The panel may have simple patterns, birds, flowers or patriotic motifs.

Dials
Dials are cut from thin sheet metal, but there are some wooden dials. The dial always has a white-painted ground.

The maker's label
The maker's name may be stamped on the movement. More often, it is on a label on the case interior. Few dials are signed.

Movements
All American shelf clocks are spring-driven, and have an anchor escapement. They are of 30-hour and eight-day duration, and strike the hours on a coiled wire gong. They are reasonably reliable timekeepers. Movements are of light construction, with stamped wheels and cut-out, rather than solid, plates, stamped from thin brass. The gong is struck by a hammer.
* The movement is always screwed to the backboard.
* On some early shelf clocks, the movement is almost entirely made of wood, with only the pivots made of metal (usually steel). Wooden movements were not necessarily less accurate than metal, as hard woods were used.

Value
Shelf clocks are decorative rather than mechanically complex. Recently, prices have risen on both sides of the Atlantic. They are rare in Europe, as a result of demand in the United States.

Certain features increase the value of a shelf clock. The clock shown *above*, made c.1825 by Joseph Ives, has a wagon-spring – a large flat leaf spring used to power the movement – also found on the clock in the main picture. The spring is housed in the wide bottom section. Ives produced these clocks in Brooklyn from c.1825.

BRACKET CASES

The earliest English bracket clock cases were usually veneered with ebony, and had an architectural top. Walnut veneer became popular from the early 18thC. Mahogany took over as the standard veneer c.1740.

Early cases often have elaborate metal mounts. From c.1725 the arched dial replaced the square dial. Arched-dial brackets became increasingly decorative in the 18thC. However, the bell top remained

Walnut c.1675
ht 19in/48cm

Ebony c.1685
ht 11¼in/29cm

Ebony c.1685
ht 13½in/34cm

Walnut c.1685
ht 14in/35.5cm

Ebony c.1695
ht 16in/41cm

Ebony c.1690
ht 15in/38.5cm

Ebony c.1760
ht 19½in/49.5cm

Walnut c.1760
ht 17½in/44cm

Mahogany c.1765
ht 18in/46cm

Ebonized c.1760
ht 21in/53cm

Lacquer c.1770
ht 25in/63.5cm

Mahogany c.1780
ht 19½in/49.5cm

the most common style.

Lacquer finishes were popular c.1730-80. These cases are among the most attractive of all English bracket clocks. Ebonized cases, typically with a bell top (or inverted bell), were also produced in the late 18thC.

In the Regency period, rosewood became fashionable, and English makers produced a great variety of case shapes. From the 1840s, inexpensive shelf clocks were imported from the United States.

The French were also prolific makers, favouring cases of gilt metal, often combined with marble or other materials.

Ebonized c.1780
ht 17in/43cm

Mahogany c.1780
ht 20½in/52cm

Mahogany c.1795
ht 15¾in/40cm

Ebonized c.1800
ht 15in/38cm

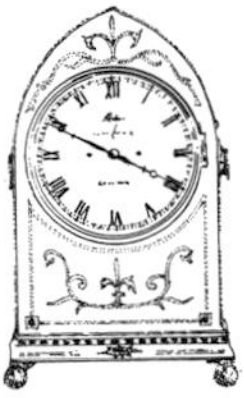

Ebonized c.1810
ht 19in/48cm

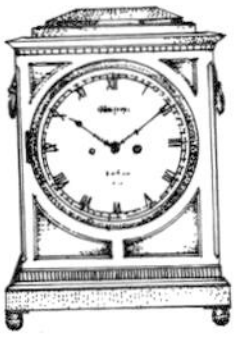

Mahogany c.1810
ht 16in/40.5cm

Gilt bronze c.1840
ht 18¾in/47.5cm

Mahogany c.1827
ht 26in/66cm

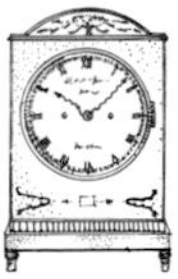

Mahogany c.1840
ht 13in/33.5cm

Mahogany c.1840
ht 19in/48cm

Mahogany c.1850
ht 18in/46cm

Ormolu c.1875
ht 18¾in/46.5cm

TAVERN CLOCKS

A tavern clock by Caleb Evans of Bristol, c.1780

Tavern clocks are large, very accurate timepieces, originally produced for taverns and coaching inns from c.1730. They are often referred to as "Act of Parliament" clocks; in 1797, an English Act of Parliament levied a tax of five shillings per year on all clocks. The tax was repealed one year later, but it led to the belief in the 20thC that tavern clocks were placed in public view because private ownership of timepieces was too costly. However, tavern clocks predate the act by several decades.

By the early 19thC, the demand for a prominent wall-hung timekeeper declined. By the time railways were built, the dial clock (see pp.98-9) was in greater demand. Very rarely, a tavern clock still hangs in its original tavern or inn.

Tavern clocks were always hung on a wall, so that they could be easily seen from a distance. The wide, clearly marked dial made them easy to read in the dim and smoky atmosphere of a tavern or inn. Tavern clocks average around

22-30in/56-76cm in diameter across the dial, and around 60in/152cm from the bottom of the trunk to the top of the dial. Smaller clocks were placed in the servant's quarters, kitchens or library of large private houses.

The earliest tavern clocks have a black shield-shaped dial with a flat bottom, supported by "wings" on the trunk. On later shield-dial tavern clocks, the bottom of the dial tapers to join the trunk. From c.1760, the round black dial and the round white dial, both with a long trunk section, are more common. Those with a white dial may have a banjo- or teardrop-shaped case. There are some miniatures, generally around 34-36in/86-91cm in height, with a lacquered case and a round white dial. The white dial indicates a late 18thC clock, and will invariably have a black chapter ring. Almost without exception, tavern clock dials do not have a bezel or a glass cover; the weight of a bezel and glass would have been too great for the wooden dial surround.

Cases are almost invariably made of oak, generally covered with lacquer decoration. Lacquer work usually followed traditional Chinoiserie style. Occasionally, the trunk section will have a coloured print applied to the door, typically showing a pastoral scene. The rarest clocks show a pub interior or a drinking scene. Mahogany veneer was used for many cases from c.1780. Lacquer decoration disappeared by c.1790, and mahogany was not used after c.1805.

All tavern clocks are weight-driven and of eight-day duration. The weights and long pendulum are contained in the trunk section. Nearly all examples are timepieces; any striking mechanism will strike only the hours.

Tavern clocks are large enough for the long pendulum to beat true seconds (see p.11). The pendulum rod is either a steel rod or a flat brass strip, with a brass-faced bob at the bottom. The weights are usually lead – sometimes brass-cased – and often oval in shape. Miniatures have wider and shallower weights to provide enough running time.

Because they were out of fashion for many years, tavern clocks suffered a long period of neglect. Dials have been damaged by amateur restoration of white dial grounds, chapter ring and signature. Lacquer decoration may have suffered damage if the clock has been too close to a fire or in direct sunlight. Movements are usually intact and in good condition, although there are examples where the striking movement from a longcase has been substituted.

Tavern clocks have been seriously collected since the late 1960s. The rarest type are the earliest shield-dial clocks, of which few were made, and even fewer have survived. Clocks with a print applied to the trunk door are the most desirable of the later tavern clocks.

Tavern clocks are workaday pieces, but look spectacular in the right setting. Most makers are not well known, as the majority of clocks were produced locally – mainly in southern England – for nearby taverns or inns. Fine examples were produced in London by Justin Vulliamy, John Dwerrihouse, and Dwerrihouse and partners.

A shield-dial tavern clock by Thomas Bucknall c.1745; ht 58in/147cm; value code B/C

Identification checklist for shield-dial tavern clocks
1. Does the clock have an arched top?
2. Is it signed prominently on the dial?
3. Is the case made of oak, with a pine or oak backboard?
4. Does it feature any Chinoiserie decoration?
5. Are there any finials? (or, if not, signs that they were once present)
6. Are the hands made of brass and fairly elaborate?
7. Is there a five-minute circle, as well as hour divisions?
8. Are there any gilt or gold leaf spandrels in the corners of the dial?
9. Is the weight made of lead? (or, more rarely, iron)

Shield-dial tavern clocks
The earliest tavern clocks – those with a shield-shaped dial – were produced from c.1730-60. They were placed in coaching inns, where accuracy was important, and in taverns. Tavern clocks are large – to be read easily – and are prominently signed on the unglazed dial.

Movements

Most tavern clocks are of eight-day duration. All are weight-driven, with a long pendulum. They are usually timepieces only. A few are of 14-day duration.

* Some movements will have been replaced with one from a longcase clock. This affects value dramatically, but is easy to detect: longcases have four holes in the frontplate to take the dial feet. Tavern dials are fixed to the case, and the movements are screwed to a seatboard; four spare holes may mean a replaced movement.

Decoration

Typically, the early tavern clocks feature Chinoiserie decoration, usually with raised gesso work on the door. The trunk interior is always plain wood.

* The corners of the dial usually have gilt spandrels.
* Shield-dials typically feature two or three gilt finials, although these have often been lost. If finials have broken off, the fixing holes will still be visible.

Early shield-dial clocks have supporting brackets or sidepieces underneath the dial. The sidepieces of the early example *above*, produced c.1720, show signs of restoration. On some clocks, the sidepieces may have broken off, leaving a "shadow" or outline on the case.

Hands

Hands are usually brass, with rounded rather than square edges. Brass may be identified by its pitted surface. The clock in the main picture has counterweights on both hands. Usually, only the minute hand has a counterweight.

Condition

* Shrinkage may cause the joints in the boards of the dial of a shield-dial clock to open up or crack (see p.93).
* Weights are usually made of lead. Replaced weights are fairly easy to detect, as lead is difficult to age artificially.

On later shield-dials, like that *above*, c.1750, the curved lower sides of the dial line up with the trunk moulding. Shaped bases are single, as here, or double (see left). Only about 50 percent of tavern clocks have their original base: the line on which the weight is suspended often broke, causing the weight to fall through the base. Good replacements are shaped. Some clocks have no base or just a piece of wood nailed across the bottom.

A round-dial tavern clock by William Stevens c.1775; ht 58in/147cm; value code C

Identification checklist for round-dial tavern clocks
1. Is the clock made of oak, with a pine or oak backboard?
2. Does it feature any lacquered Chinoiserie decoration?
3. Is the clock signed at the top of the trunk?
4. Is there a five-minute ring on the dial?
5. Does the top of the trunk feature any applied "ears"?
6. Are the hands made of brass?
7. On black round dials, is the chapter ring picked out in gold leaf?
8. On white round dials, is the chapter ring painted black on white-painted, gessoed wood?

Round-dials
Tavern clocks with round dials made their appearance in the 1750s. The earliest, which are now very rare, feature a black dial. The clock in the main picture, produced c.1775, is typical. The white-painted round dial was introduced c.1780 and was produced until c.1800. As on

shield-dials (see pp.90-1), the trunk doors of round-dial tavern clocks most commonly feature lacquered Chinoiserie decoration.
* The applied sidepieces, or "ears", at the base of the dial sides are characteristic of these clocks. They are fairly delicate, and may have been repaired.
* The brass hands are usually tipped by hearts. Some hands will have simple piercing.

This tavern clock, *above*, produced c.1780, is only 35½in/90cm in height, and so is much smaller than most other round-dials. The crazing (fine cracks) on the dial, just visible in this picture, shows the age of the piece and blends with the fine lacquer decoration on the trunk. Crazing does not detract from value.
* The covered winding hole indicates high quality, and is a refinement found on some round-dials (but not on shield-dials).

Movements
All examples are weight-driven, with an anchor escapement. Most have a long pendulum. They are typically of eight-day duration. Movements will never be identical in layout.
* If a movement has been replaced, perhaps by one from a longcase clock (see p.91), a new winding hole may have been made in the dial, and the old hole blocked off.
* Any round-dial which strikes the hours is very rare.

Signatures
Round-dial clocks are prominently signed under the dial at the top of the trunk (instead of on the dial itself).

This white round-dial clock, *above*, produced c.1780, features a well-preserved print, showing a tavern scene, applied to the trunk door. Such decoration is relatively rare and any clocks with a tavern scene are highly sought-after. Because of the effects of tavern smoke, the dial has darkened, giving the piece a natural mellow finish which should not be cleaned off.

Condition
As with all tavern clocks, the case should be structurally sound. On clocks with white round-dials, the bottom section of the trunk should be intact (see p.91). Look for cracks caused by shrinkage in the painted dial and its surround.
* On white round-dials, the numerals were painted in black on the painted and gessoed wooden dial. Black dials always have gold leaf numerals. Because the dial did not have a glass cover, the numerals on the chapter ring of tavern clocks inevitably suffer wear. Some repainting of the chapter ring and signature is acceptable, but a wholly repainted ground can dramatically reduce the value of a tavern clock.

A banjo-case tavern clock by J. Bartholomew c.1780; ht 56in/142cm; value code C

Identification checklist for banjo-case tavern clocks
1. Does the clock have a round white dial?
2. Does the banjo-shaped case have lacquered Chinoiserie decoration?
3. Is it signed at the top of the trunk?
4. On clocks with a wide trunk section, is the trunk door of lift-out pattern, rather than hinged?
5. Is there a five-minute ring on the dial?
6. Does the case have "ear pieces"? (see below)
7. Are the hands made of brass?

Banjo-case tavern clocks
Taking their name from the shape of the trunk, banjo-cases are one of the most distinctive types of tavern clock. The proportions of the case vary, but in other respects, these timepieces are very similar to white round-dial tavern clocks. All are of eight-day duration. They generally feature traditional Chinoiserie decoration on the trunk door, a white-painted dial and brass hands (often tipped with hearts). Banjo-cases are signed at the top of the trunk. This type of tavern clock was not produced in great numbers.

Applied decoration
The clock in the main picture has large decorative ears applied to the sides of the trunk just under the dial. This was a feature common to ordinary round dials as well. If a clock has no ear pieces, look for glue marks or a "shadow" where the ears and their supporting wood blocks might have been.

Like the clock in the main picture, the example *above*, produced by the Liverpool maker Joseph Finney c.1770, has a particularly pronounced banjo shape. At 62in/157cm in height, this clock is unusually large. Because of the shape of the case, the trunk doors of banjo tavern clocks were often difficult to hinge. On this clock, the door lifts out, and two pegs at the bottom engage with the frame. The door can then be locked in place. On some later cases, the door is straight-sided.

Makers
Tavern clocks were produced by a host of makers all over England, but mostly based in the southeast. The name on a clock indicates the seller of the piece, who also made the movement but generally bought the case from a separate cabinetmaker.

The banjo shape of the c.1785 example *above*, is less pronounced than that of the clock in the main picture, and so features a hinged door. This style was favoured by the maker, Justin Vulliamy.

Mahogany tavern clocks
Tavern clocks with mahogany cases were produced c.1790-1810. All have a round white signed dial, and the same style of movement and pendulum as on earlier examples.

Mahogany cases are shorter than lacquered cases, and may have a hinged bottom. The example *above*, made by Dwerrihouse c.1800, is 43in/109cm in height.

WALL CLOCKS

A Louis XV gilt bronze cartel clock signed "Bunon à Paris", c.1760

The term "wall clock" simply means any clock – either weight- or spring-driven – that is hung on a wall. It embraces a wide variety of styles, from the simplicity of the English round-dial clock, to the exuberantly carved German cuckoo clock and the ornately-cast metal cartel clock.

In England, the basic round-dial clock was introduced in the 1770s. Its forerunner was the later versions of the tavern clock (see pp.88-95). The inexpensive round-dial clock came about as a result of Britain's increasing wealth, which created a growing demand for timekeepers. The round-dial clock, and its major variant, the trunk-dial, were intended to be useful rather than decorative. They are simple in appearance, and easily read. Produced from c.1785, trunk-dial clocks were probably made for the study or library of clubs or large private houses.

The cases of English wall clocks are almost invariably mahogany. On round-dial clocks, solid mahogany was used.

This is usually not as finely figured as on many bracket and longcase clocks, as little of the case is visible. The cases of trunk-dial wall clocks may be very finely figured, and the best examples may be inlaid and strung with brass.

English wall clocks are mainly timepieces, and rarely strike the hours. All are spring-driven, and typically have a fusee movement (see p.11). Early round-dial clocks had a verge escapement (see p.10), with a short pendulum. From the late 18thC, wall clocks were fitted with more accurate anchor escapements. Because of the longer pendulum required, the case was extended to form the trunk.

The earliest English dials are painted wood, and either flat or convex. On the very rare early examples, the dial ground is painted black, with gilt numerals. However, most dial clocks on the market today have an engraved and silvered brass dial, or a white-painted wood or iron dial. Early examples are convex in shape. Those made from c.1840 are flat. The dial is always glazed, with a brass bezel.

The first competition to the English wall clocks came from the wooden clocks produced in the Black Forest region of Germany. Clockmaking in the Black Forest began in the 17thC as a source of extra income for local people during the winter months. The industry flourished in the 18thC and underwent intensive development during the early 19thC, when large numbers of Black Forest clocks were exported.

Black Forest clocks are all weight-driven, and almost all are of 30-hour duration. They are easily wound; the weights are simply pulled up every night. From the late 18thC, all Black Forest clocks had an anchor escapement (see p.10). Most strike the hours, and later ones may have an alarm – an inexpensive and convenient feature. Like the cases, the movements of early Black Forest clocks were made largely of wood. In the 19thC, mass-produced brass and steel movements were standard.

Black Forest clocks often have additional features, such as musical work or automaton figures. Figures appear in a cut-out on the painted wood dial. With its richly carved case, the cuckoo clock is the most famous type of Black Forest clock. It is wrongly considered to be a Swiss invention.

Wall clocks were produced in the United States from c.1780. From c.1850, exports of inexpensive American wall clocks contributed to the decline in popularity of English wall clocks. All American wall clocks are weight-driven, with an anchor escapement and a long pendulum with a brass bob. Typical features include a white-painted metal dial, as well as a panel of *verre eglomisé* (reverse-painted glass). The "banjo" case is the most sought-after American wall clock.

The cartel clock – a decorative spring-driven wall clock with a cast metal case – was produced from the late 18thC, mainly in France. French cartel clocks are all of eight-day duration, with a verge escapement and a going barrel (see p.11) rather than a fusee. Most have a convex enamel dial. English cartels have carved and gilded wooden cases (instead of metal) and are highly sought after today.

ROUND-DIAL WALL CLOCKS

A round-dial wall clock by Richard Ward c.1780; ht 16in/41cm; value code D/E

Identification checklist for round-dial wall clocks
1. Is the case mahogany?
2. Does it have a bottom door and at least one side door?
3. Does it have a mellow appearance? (indicative of age)
4. On early clocks, does the back have a "saltbox"? (see below)
5. If there is a painted dial, is it in good condition?
6. Does the dial have a glass cover?
7. Is the clock signed?
8. Are the hands blued steel? (or, more rarely, brass)

Round-dial wall clocks
Round-dial wall clocks, known as English dial clocks, were first produced during the 1750s. Most were made in London, but large quantities were produced in East Anglia and major southern towns. Round-dials are functional, rather than decorative, although many are fairly elegant in appearance. They were typically placed in offices and shops. Little of the case, which is usually mahogany, is visible, so well-figured veneer is not as important as it is for other types of case.

The "saltbox"
Until c.1780, round-dial wall clocks were fixed to the wall by means of a backboard known as a "saltbox", shown *opposite, top*, attached to the back of the case. The saltbox had a hole in the top (and sometimes the bottom), through which the clock could be fixed to the wall. On the clock in the main picture, the top and "tail" (bottom) of the saltbox are just visible. On later clocks, a brass plate was let into the back of the case, so that the clock could be hung on a hook.

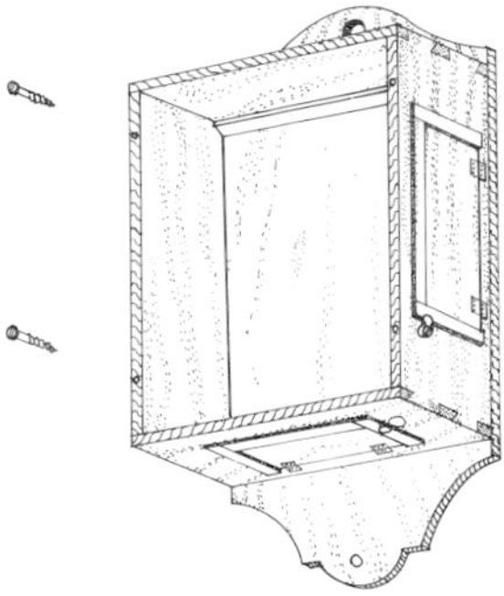

* All wall clocks have a door in the bottom and one in the side of the case, to provide access to the pendulum and the movement. Clocks which strike the hours have two side doors.

Movements
Most round-dial wall clocks are simple timepieces. Possibly because a striking train makes a clock more expensive, it is rare to find a striking wall clock. Round-dial wall clocks are always of eight-day duration, with fusee movement (see p.11).
* On the piece in the main picture, the dial is screwed to the wooden surround. On the best wall clocks the movement is fixed to a seatboard screwed into the case. In this way, no screw holes are visible on the dial.

Round-dial wall clocks made in the 18thC typically have a verge escapement. The movement *above* shows the horizontally-mounted escape wheel at the top and the short pendulum. Also visible is the conical fusee movement. Wall clocks made after 1800 generally have an anchor escapement (see p.10).

Dials
Dials may be wood, silvered brass or iron, and either convex or flat. The most common size is 12in/30.5cm, like that of the clock in the main picture. The largest dial size is 20in/51cm.
* Some crazing (fine cracks) is acceptable on a painted wood or iron dial, but chipping or scratching is not.

Early dials are convex, and are solid wood. However, the c.1745 dial *above* consists of three sections. Wood and iron dials are painted white (with black numerals) or, rarely, black (with gold numerals). The best iron dials were made c.1805-50.

The late wall clock, *above*, made by John Moore c.1860, has a serial number. Few makers numbered their clocks.
* The bezel of earlier clocks is cast brass, and closes with a tag or lock. Later wall clocks may have a bezel of much lighter spun brass.
* Hands are usually blued steel; some are brass. Spade- or heart-tipped hands (plain or pierced) were popular.

TRUNK-DIAL WALL CLOCKS

A trunk-dial wall clock by Matthew & Thomas Dutton c.1800; ht 26in/66cm; value code D

Identification checklist for trunk-dial wall clocks
1. Does the trunk have two doors?
2. Is the mahogany veneer of good figuring?
3. If there is a painted dial, is the white ground free of cracks and scratches?
4. Is there a glass cover to the dial?
5. Is the clock signed?
6. Are the hands blued steel? (or, rarely, brass)

Trunk-dial wall clocks
Taking their name from the trunk or box below the dial, trunk-dial wall clocks began to appear from c.1785. The trunk allowed the clock to take a longer pendulum, a feature which improved their accuracy. However, the main reason for the addition of the trunk may have been aesthetic, as decorative features like the shaped "ears" on the piece in the main picture could be added. In contrast to round-dial wall clocks, the mahogany veneer on trunk-dial clocks is generally well figured. The trunk panelling on the clock in the main picture is a feature unique to its makers.

* Movements are identical to those of round-dials (see p.99). Most are timepieces only; striking clocks are rare.

* The majority of trunk-dial wall clocks were produced by makers in London or other cities in southeast England.
* Hands are made of brass or blued steel.

As well as a side door, the trunk always has a bottom door. On the clock *above*, made c.1805 by Benjamin Vulliamy, the bottom slopes back – a feature known as a chisel foot. The foot may be elaborately shaped.
* Trunk-dials are hung using a hook or a cut-out.

Dials
Dials may be convex or flat, and made of painted wood or iron, or silvered brass. They are usually 12in/30cm in diameter.

At 17in/43cm, the painted wood dial of the clock *above*, made by Barber of Bristol c.1785, is unusually large. The two winding holes show that it strikes the hours. The five-minute ring is typical of early dial clocks.

The clock *above*, made in 1843, also by Benjamin Vulliamy, is unusual, as it has a date and a number, as well as a signature. Vulliamy was one of the few makers to number his clocks.
* Screws visible on the dial secure the dial feet, which are fixed to the movement. As an alternative to screws, the feet may be riveted to the dial and should be barely visible.
* A visible catch on the bezel usually indicates a replaced lock; this is unlikely to affect value.

With its three finials and elaborately pierced fretwork, this rare mahogany wall clock, *above*, made by Alexander Cumming c.1780, recalls the hood of a longcase clock rather than a wall clock.

A "double decker" wall clock by Seth Thomas c.1860; ht 34in/86cm; value code F

Identification checklist for American wall clocks

1. Is the case either mahogany or rosewood?
2. Does it have a painted glass panel? (the best have two)
3. Does the clock have a painted metal dial?
4. Does it have an anchor escapement, with a brass pendulum bob?
5. Does the movement have a maker's stamp?
6. Is there a maker's card stuck to the inside of the case?
7. Does the clock have black-painted steel hands?

American wall clocks
Most American wall clocks were made c.1840-80, by such well-known makers as Seth Thomas and Chauncey Jerome. These mass-produced weight-driven clocks are well-made. They were widely exported, and their low prices made them popular. Many have now been shipped back to the United States.
* There are two brass hanging plates on the back.

Cases
Case styles include the "OG", the "double decker" and the "beehive". The "banjo" case is the most famous (see right). Mahogany was the most common case veneer, but many cases are veneered with the more costly rosewood. The gilded columns and two painted-glass picture doors on the rosewood "double decker" clock in the main picture are indicative of quality.

The OG (or ogee) clock took its name from the shape of the moulding around the dial and door. Unusually, the walnut-veneered example *above*, made by Chauncey Jerome c.1860, has two front doors. Most wall clocks have one. Although there are some OG clocks of eight-day duration, most run for 30 hours.

Glass panels
Panels of *verre eglomisé* (reverse-painted glass) are typical: they show animals, plants, famous places or people, or patterns. Broken panels reduce value: replacements are plain glass.

Movements
All examples have an anchor escapement (see p.10) and strike the hours (on a gong). They are of eight-day or 30-hour duration. Movements were machine-stamped. Weights hang inside the case (rather than out from the bottom as on other wall clocks).

Signatures
American wall clocks typically have a card stuck to the back of the case interior, bearing the maker's name and, sometimes, simple instructions on the operation of the clock. The movement usually bears the stamp of the maker.

The banjo case
Patented by Simon Willard in 1802, the banjo case is one of the most sought-after types of 19thC American wall clocks. They were made in Connecticut, but not in large numbers, and so are rare today. Banjo clocks are most commonly timepieces rather than striking clocks. They are weight-driven, with lead or iron weights.
* Dials are usually convex, painted metal.
* There is usually a maker's label stuck to the case interior.

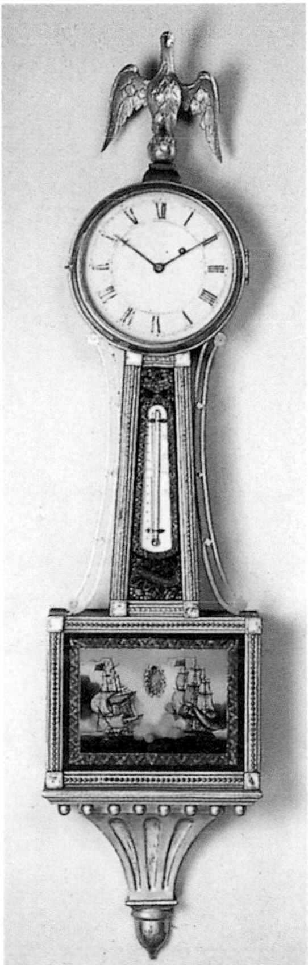

The shape and size of banjo cases are standard, but surface decoration varies widely. On the early 19thC example *above*, with a gilded case and thermometer, the lower section has a reverse-painted glass panel. The square or rectangular lower section is typical of wooden banjo cases. Variations such as the *Girandole* have a round one. The "rails" flanking the middle section are found on all banjo cases.

A rare early "cow tail" Black Forest pendulum clock c.1740; ht 12in/30cm; value code D/E

Identification checklist for Black Forest clocks

1. Is the movement made of wood? (pre-1790 only)
2. Is the dial made of a single piece of wood, and decorated with painted flowers? (or, with a *repoussé* metal surround)
3. Is the clock weight-driven?
4. Are the weights iron?
5. Does the clock strike on a bell?
6. Does it feature any automata? (late 18th and early 19thC)
7. Is the movement housed in an unfinished wooden box?
8. Is the back solid, with two side doors?
9. Does the dial show any signs of cracking?
10. Are the hands brass? (or, rarely, wood)

Black Forest clocks
Clockmaking in the Black Forest region of southwest Germany began in the late 17thC, but did not flourish until after the Treaty of Utrecht (1713). Because of the region's abundance of trees, early Black Forest clocks are invariably made of wood. Initially, makers worked only during the winter;

however, by 1740, a major industry had been set up. At first, these inexpensive clocks were sold locally by pedlars, but during the 19thC they were widely exported.

* The movement is housed in a box of crudely finished wood. It is solid at the back and has two side doors.
* Black Forest clocks are wall-hung, by means of a hook or loop at the top of the box. There are also two feet at the bottom of the box to keep it vertical.
* Brass hands are common, but early ones may be carved wood.

Movements

Almost without exception, Black Forest clocks are weight-driven, and of 30-hour duration, and so must be wound every day. Early clocks may be either striking or simple timepieces. From the late 18thC, most were fitted with an anchor escapement, with a long pendulum. Examples with a front-swinging pendulum, like the one shown left, are rare. Even sophisticated pieces are not accurate timekeepers.

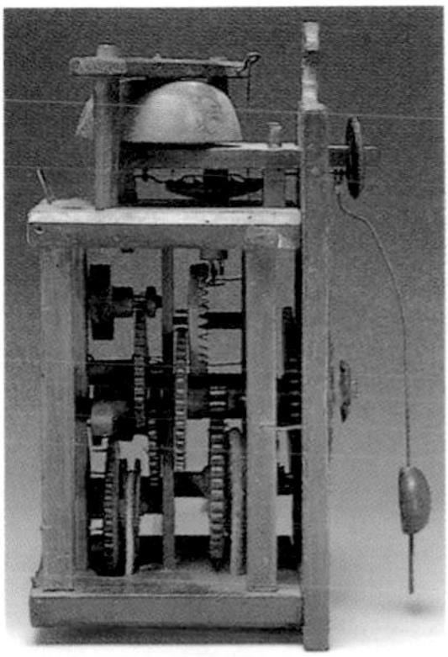

The movements of early Black Forest clocks were made mainly of wood. In the movement *above*, from the clock in the main picture, the only metal parts are the pinions, the bell and the pallets on the verge escapement.

Signatures

Black Forest clocks are rarely signed on the dial, unless by a retailer. A maker's signature may be on the back or on one of the side doors.

"Complications", such as musical work or automata, are common. On the clock *above*, made by the Christian Wehrle family c.1800, the three-train movement strikes the hours and plays one of six tunes by means of hammers striking zither strings.

Black Forest clocks of the late 18thC usually have a painted wood shield dial. As on the c.1800 example *above*, the dial may also have a cut-out with automaton figures.

Condition

Examine the clock carefully: the wooden plates, movements and dial often suffer from wear or woodworm. The dial may shrink and split, and the pull of the weights can distort the frame.

19thC Black Forest Clocks
By the 19thC, Black Forest clocks were being made with steel or brass movements (but often with wooden plates). Most are of 30-hour duration with an anchor escapement, but there are some of eight-day duration. The pendulum rod is steel, although the bob is often a brass disc or wood sheathed in brass. The painted shield was the most common dial. Some dials have carved or *repoussé* (hammered) metal decoration. Black Forest clocks from this period are more common than 18thC ones, and are more affordable.
* 19thC Black Forest clocks are practically never signed.

During the 19thC, Black Forest clocks found markets in Scandinavia, Britain and elsewhere in Europe. The "tartan" shield-dial clock *above*, produced c.1820, may have been intended for the Scottish market. Fruit and flower motifs, often of high quality, feature in the arch of early painted shield-dials. On late 19thC clocks, decoration is more standardized.
* Shield-dials are usually of 30-hour duration.
* Dials of 19thC clocks are invariably made of wood.

The pedlar was a popular subject for Black Forest miniatures. As on the 14in/36.5cm-high example *above*, the painted tin figures hold a set of pendulums and a shield-dial clock. This figure holds a spring-driven timepiece. These clocks are rare.
* There are some fakes, made of cast metal, not tin.

Miniature alarm timepieces, like the one shown *above*, were made by Josef Sorg in Neustadt from c.1800, and are extremely rare today. *Sorguhr* (Sorg clocks) have brass-cased weights and a *repoussé* brass cresting over the 2⅓in/6cm porcelain dial.
* Most Black Forest clocks have two iron weights.

* Clocks with alarms were popular in the late 19thC. The so-called "Postman's Alarm" (still found on the English market), resembles an English round-dial clock (see pp.98-9).

Condition
Through wear, the wooden plates of Black Forest clocks can loosen and drop "out of square". They may also be attacked by woodworm (see p.59).

Clocks with automata or musical work were popular throughout the 19thC. The trumpeter clock, *above*, produced c.1890, sounds the hours on four metal trumpets worked by bellows, while the door below the dial reveals a guardsman. Trumpeter clocks were made from c.1850.
* Other 19thC variations include picture clocks, with painted or *repoussé* metal dial surrounds. Animal scenes are common: on some, the animals' eyes move as the clock ticks.
* Hands and figures carved from bone, as on this clock, are also common on cuckoo clocks.

The cuckoo clock
The cuckoo clock was made in the Black Forest from c.1850 until World War II. The carved pine case has a gabled roof, and a back flap to allow access to the movement.
* Cases should be carefully inspected to ensure that carvings are intact.

Most cuckoo clocks are weight-driven and wall-hanging. There are some spring-driven shelf-standing examples, like the musical and automaton clock shown *above*. The cuckoo call accompanies a bell or gong. Only the best ones have both musical and automaton work. The cuckoo is made of painted wood: the finest have moveable wings and beak.

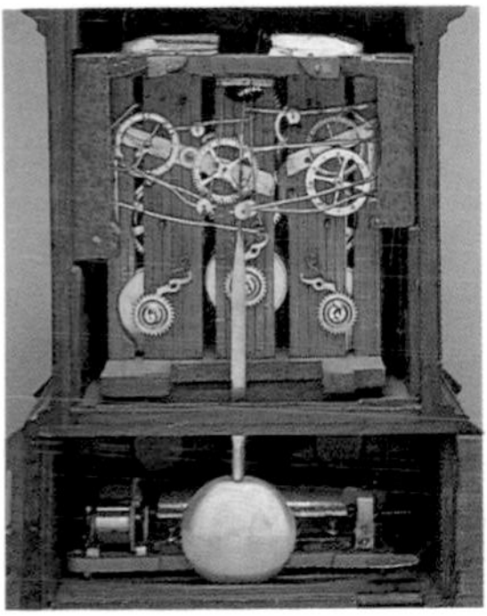

The wooden plates of the movement from the cuckoo clock above, are typical. The twin bellows above the plates, which produce the "cuckoo" call, were originally made of chicken skin. This can wear out or develop leaks, and so has often been replaced (with no effect on value).

A French ormolu cartel clock by Chevrau c.1780; ht 29in/74cm; value code D/E

Identification checklist for French cartel clocks
1. Does the clock have a gilded metal case? (probably cast brass)
2. Is the case highly decorative in appearance? (with detailed scrolling, cherubs and foliage)
3. Is the dial enamel?
4. Does the clock strike the hours?
5. Is the back unfinished?
6. Are the hands elaborately pierced?
7. Is the dial (and possibly the movement) signed?

French cartel clocks
The word "cartel" may come from the Italian *cartella*, or wall bracket, and refers to decorative, spring-driven wall clocks produced mainly in France during the second half of the 18thC. There are some early

19thC cartels on the market. Cartel clocks were very popular in France, and makers produced many variations on the basic style. English makers also produced distinctive examples (see right). Cartel clocks are prized for their visual appeal.

The case
The cases of French cartel clocks are invariably made of intricately cast ormolu (brass with a gilded finish). Like the clock in the main picture, they generally have elaborate decorative features, such as figures, female masks, sunburst rays, scrolling foliage and Classical urns.

Being of cast metal, the case is very strong, allowing makers to cast crisp, detailed scenes. The asymmetrical cherubs and foliage on the c.1750 cartel *above*, are typical. Cases usually survive well, and only need to be dusted.
* The dial is usually signed. The movement may also be signed.

Movements
All cartels are spring-driven, and of eight-day duration. French examples have a verge escapement (see p.10). Most strike the hours; some may strike the quarter-hours. They have a going barrel (see p.11).
* A door in the back provides access to the movement.

Dials
The enamel dial may be chipped near the winding holes due to careless use of the winding key.

On the unusual Swiss cartel *above*, produced c.1780, the numerals are set vertically on the convex enamel dial, rather than in their usual positions on the chapter ring. Swiss cartels are rare; most cartels are Paris-made.

English cartel clocks
English cartels were made in small numbers c.1730-70. They are highly collectable, especially if the case is in good condition.

Cases are of carved and gilded wood, as on the c.1760 example *above*. They are easily damaged; those with original gilding, even if weathered, are sought after. Regilded cases appear bright and of uniform finish.

REGULATORS

A flat-topped mahogany longcase regulator by John Holmes c.1780

The regulator is an extremely accurate weight-driven clock – either wall-hung or floor-standing – used as a standard of timekeeping for other clocks. Regulators were produced in England and in France from the mid-18thC to around the end of the 19thC. The regulators produced by Viennese makers in the early 19thC are dealt with in a separate section (see pp.152-61).

A regulator was usually found in the workshop of a clockmaker and in the shop of an important retailer. Large private houses with many clocks would also probably have owned at least one. If the size of the collection justified it, the local clockmaker would visit every week to wind the clocks and adjust the settings, using the time indicated by the household's regulator.

The case of the English floor-standing, or longcase regulator closely resembles that of a longcase clock. It provides a stable, dust-free environment to house the clock movement, the weight and the long pendulum. Cases are nearly always mahogany, although there are a few examples in oak. They are well-made and of solid construction, and were generally screwed to a wall to reduce the effects of vibration.

Cases are plainer than those of longcase clocks, as the regulator was intended to fulfil a useful, rather than a decorative role. Even so, regulator cases can look very handsome.

The earliest English longcase regulators have an architectural top and a solid, veneered trunk door. Those made after c.1820 often have a glazed door (and a rounded top). Regulators from the late 19thC may not be as visually appealing as late 18th or early 19thC examples.

The regulator dial has a unique layout, designed to allow the time to be accurately read. The dial is almost invariably round and made of engraved and silvered brass. Minutes and seconds are shown more prominently than hours, as the regulator was used for fine regulation rather than general timekeeping. On a standard clock dial, the hour divisions are prominent on the chapter ring. A regulator shows minutes on the chapter ring, and seconds on a subsidiary dial above the dial centre. Hours are shown on a subsidiary dial or aperture below the dial centre.

Regulator movements are very finely made. They have no striking mechanism, and so only one weight. In order to keep accurate time and reduce friction in the train, regulators commonly incorporate technical refinements such as jewelled pallets or jewelled pivots. Most regulators have maintaining power (see p.175), which ensures that the clock does not stop (and lose time) during winding. To keep the clock stable and avoid any disturbance to timekeeping, the movement is fixed to a substantial seatboard.

An English regulator pendulum is more sophisticated than the standard longcase pendulum. It was intended to reduce or compensate for expansion or contraction in the length of the pendulum due to changes in temperature, which could affect the accuracy of the clock's timekeeping. The pendulum may be of the compensated "gridiron" type, a pine rod with brass bob or a steel rod with a mercury-filled glass jar as the bob (see p.11). To ensure stability, the pendulum is often suspended from a heavy backcock (see p.65) fixed to the substantial backboard. The brass-cased weight is nearly always well finished.

Wall-hanging regulators were produced from the mid-19thC, but in smaller numbers than the floor-standing type. The wall-hanging regulator takes up less space, and is prized by collectors as an elegant wall clock in its own right. Some are weight-driven, but there are many spring-driven examples with a fusee movement (see p.11). Wall-hanging regulators may be slightly less accurate than longcases.

Longcase regulators were produced in France from the late 18thC and throughout the 19thC. They were not made in large numbers. The cases of these clocks are elaborate, and often have inlaid or applied decoration. French dials are generally enamel, and convex in shape, with a more varied layout than English examples. A typical feature of French regulators is the gridiron pendulum, with large brass bob.

The relatively small number of longcase and wall-hanging regulators in circulation today reflects the fact that they were originally not intended for a wide market. They particularly appeal to those collectors interested in the development of fine precision timekeepers.

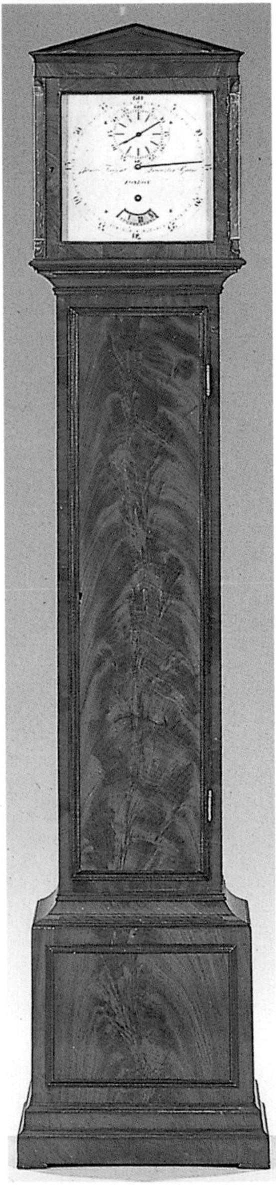

A longcase regulator by James Tregent; c.1800; ht 71in/180cm; value code B

Identification checklist for English longcase regulators
1. Is the case mahogany?
2. Is there a panelled base?
3. Does the hood slide off?
4. Does the clock have a silvered dial? (with minutes on the chapter ring and subsidiary dials for hours and seconds)
5. Does the clock have maintaining power? (see below)
6. Is it a timepiece rather than a striking clock?
7. Is it signed on the dial?
8. Are the hands blued steel, and very simple in shape?

Longcase regulators
The development of the regulator during the late 18thC arose from the need for an extremely accurate standard timekeeper by which other clocks could be set. All regulators keep virtually perfect time, and were typically used in large houses or clock workshops.

The case
Cases resemble those of domestic longcase clocks, but are usually plainer. They are almost all mahogany, and typically finely figured. The architectural top, like that on the regulator in the main picture, is most common on early longcase examples, which also feature a slide-off hood. By the mid-19thC, the rounded top was the most common style, and the solid trunk door had given way to the glazed door. Cases from this period may also be elaborately decorated. As with the best longcase clocks, bases are commonly panelled, with either a double or single plinth.

The dial
Whether square or round, regulator dials are always silvered brass, with engraved numerals filled with black wax. Most regulators have the same distinctive dial layout, with separate indications for seconds, minutes and hours. Early

regulators tend to have an aperture to display the hours, which are marked on a revolving disc under the dial. However, most 19thC regulators show the minutes on the chapter ring, with subsidiary dials showing seconds and hours.
* Hands are always blued steel and simple in shape.

Although the dialplate is typically either square or round, the shallow arched dial with pediment and three finials on top of the case is a fairly common style, as on the c.1821 example *above*. Although signed by George Leach of Kingston, Jamaica, it is likely that this regulator was commissioned from a London firm and exported.

The signature
All longcase regulators are signed on the dial, and sometimes also on the backplate.
* If a clockmaking workshop changed hands, the new owner sometimes removed the former owner's signature from the dial by hammering it out from the back. The dial would then be re-engraved with the new owner's name. This will only be apparent by removing the hood and looking at the back of the dial. A new signature does not detract from the value of a clock.

Additional features
Regulator movements are very finely made. They typically include such refinements as maintaining power, a system of springs which ensured the clock did not lose any time during winding. To reduce friction, the pallets – the metal arms which engage the teeth of the escape wheel – are often jewelled, as are many of the pivots. Most regulators are timepieces only, as the vibration caused by a striking mechanism can affect the instrument's accuracy.

If there is a glazed door, as shown on the example *above*, produced c.1850 by Benjamin Vulliamy, the pendulum is either a mercury-filled jar or, as here, a gridiron (see p.11). A wood rod is used if the trunk is solid. Wood is less subject than metal to temperature changes (which alter the length of the pendulum rod and affect accuracy). The two weights visible here indicate a striking clock – a rare feature.
* If there is a glazed door, the back of the case interior may be veneered, as it will be visible.

WALL REGULATORS

A month-duration wall-hanging regulator by Charles Frodsham c.1880; ht 49in/124cm; value code C/D

Identification checklist for wall-hanging regulators

1. Does the regulator have a mahogany-veneered case? (a few are walnut)

2. Is the regulator spring-driven? (some examples are weight-driven)

3. Is it a timepiece rather than a striking clock?

4. Does it have a mercury pendulum?

5. Is there an engraved silvered dial, with seconds shown on a subsidiary dial?

6. Is the dial signed?

7. Are the hands made of blued steel? (possibly with a *fleur-de-lys* motif on the tips)

Wall-hanging regulators
The wall-hanging version of the regulator was produced throughout the 19thC. They were made chiefly by London firms, notably Edward Dent, Charles Frodsham, Benjamin Lewis and Benjamin Vulliamy, although there are some examples by Liverpool makers. Like longcases, production of wall-hanging regulators was small, and they are not easy to find today. Any examples in circulation are usually in very good condition, partly because they were made relatively recently, but also because such an important instrument was generally well looked after.

Dial
The dial is usually silvered brass (but may be gilded), with engraved numerals, and may be either round or arched. Most have the traditional layout (see below), with simple blued steel hands. However, the clock in the main picture shows hours and minutes on the chapter ring and seconds on a subsidiary dial.

Nearly all regulator dials show minutes on the chapter ring and seconds and hours on subsidiary dials. The dial *above*, made by Charles Frodsham c.1860 is typical. The signature is usually on the dial, but may also appear on the backplate. Exhibition medals or royal appointments, as on this example, do not always indicate high quality.

The case
Cases are usually mahogany-veneered, with a flat or rounded top and glazed sides and door. Wall regulators that are spring-driven have no hanging weights, but just a long pendulum.

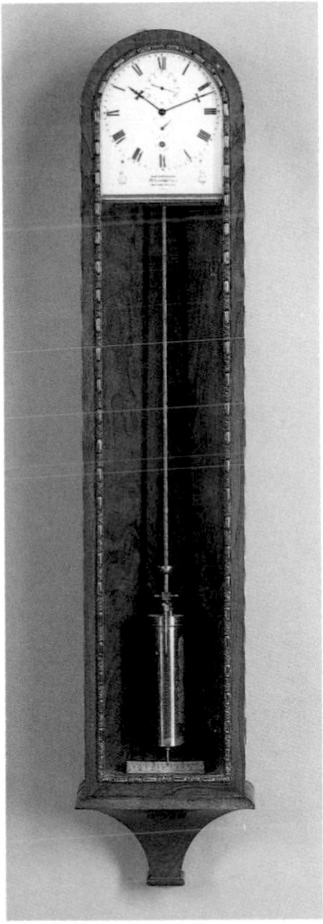

The wall regulator *above*, produced by Charles Frodsham c.1860, is unusual in being veneered with walnut (rather than mahogany).
* Height varies from as little as 45in/114cm to 55in/138cm.

Movements
Most wall regulators have a dead beat anchor escapement, with a fusee movement and maintaining power (see p.113). The best examples have jewelled pallets and pivots. Most are spring- rather than weight-driven; the case is too short for weights to fall. The clock in the main picture is of one-month duration; most are eight-day.
* The pendulum bob is usually a mercury jar (see p.11). A replaced pendulum is likely to be a steel rod with brass bob.
* The beat scale (see p.157) at the bottom of the case ensures an even pendulum swing.

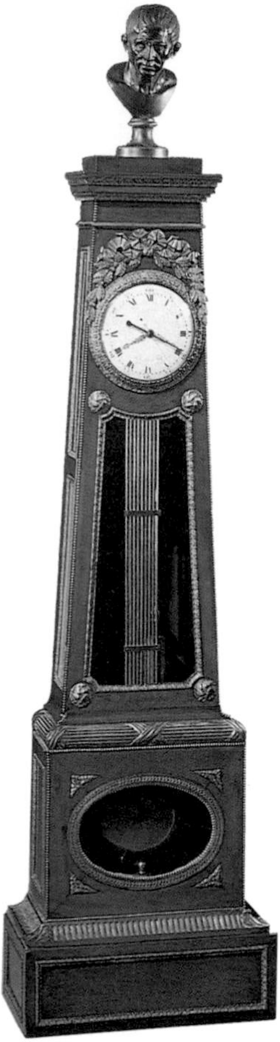

A Louis XVI longcase regulator by Raguet Lepine c.1780; ht 73½in/187cm; value code A

Identification checklist for French longcase regulators

1. Does the clock have a mahogany case?
2. Is the case square-topped? (some also have a finial)
3. Are the front and sides glazed?
4. Is the back of the case unfinished?
5. Is there a gridiron pendulum? (see below)
6. Is the dial enamelled? (silvered dials are unusual)
7. Are there any gilt bronze mouldings or mounts to the case?
8. Is the clock signed?
9. Are the hands fairly elaborate?

French regulators
Small numbers of regulators were produced by French makers – mostly Parisian – from the late 18thC, and throughout the 19thC. They are less accurate than the best English examples. The few in circulation are sought after by collectors.

Cases
Most cases are square-topped, with a large cornice. Many 18thC examples, like the clock in the main picture, have an ornate top finial. There may be a moulded base panel. Cases are usually mahogany-veneered, but there are a few in walnut. Veneers are not as well figured as on English cases.
* Bronze mouldings and mounts are characteristic features.
* The front and sides of the trunk are always glazed.
* Backs are not finely finished.

Signatures
The signature may be on the dial or on the backplate. On the clock in the main picture, the movement is signed by the maker, and the dial by the enameller.

The dial
French regulators generally have an enamelled dial with a brass bezel. The dial layout resembles that of an ordinary longcase clock (unlike English regulators, which have a specific dial layout). Hands are generally elaborate.

The dial may have a number of subsidiary dials. The detail *above*, with the dial plate removed, from a c.1851 example, shows the movements for subsidiary dials giving: day, month, year, season, solar cycle, day and phase of the moon and times of sunrise and sunset.

Movements
Most examples strike the hours (and sometimes the half-hours), on a bell or on a gong. From the mid-18thC, the pin wheel (see p.10) was the most common escape mechanism, There are some with a dead beat escapement (see p.173).

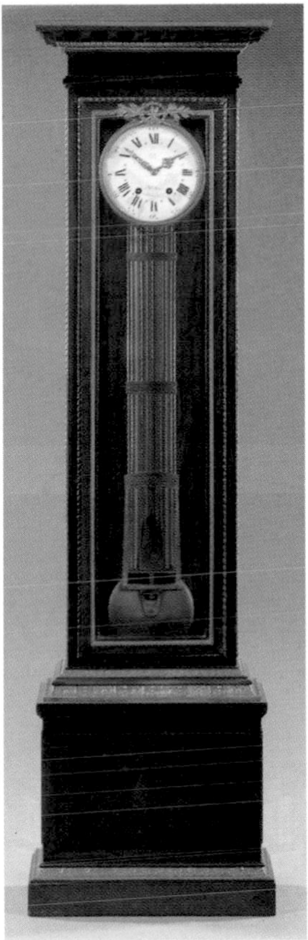

The most characteristic feature of French regulator movements is the very large gridiron pendulum. As on the c.1900 example *above*, this consists of up to nine rods of alternating brass and steel. The differing rates of expansion and contraction of these rods ensures that the length of the rod remains constant. On this example, the gridiron is unusually large. The pendulum bob is typically lead with a brass facing.

SKELETON CLOCKS

A French skeleton mantel clock with four subsidiary dials by Edouard François, c.1900

With their characteristic cut-out plates and often elaborate design, skeleton clocks are among the most fascinating of all antique clocks. The basic principle is to display as much of the working mechanism as possible. The brass frame – always pierced or heavily fretted – is essential to the appearance of a skeleton clock. All stand on a base of veneered wood or marble, with a glass dome to keep dust out of the movements.

The earliest examples were probably French, although the origins of the skeleton may lie with Austrian clocks. However, it was in England that the skeleton clock underwent the greatest development. The first English skeleton clocks were produced c.1820, and were made until c.1870. The earliest examples are simple, but later they became very complex, often incorporating architectural motifs and elaborate striking mechanisms.

The plates of a skeleton clock are always brass, and always cut out from solid cast sheets. There are no stamped plates. Even late 19thC skeleton plates are finely engineered and finished. Plates are secured to their pillars by small blued steel screws, and are finished with a clear lacquer.

Skeleton clocks were made by many leading English makers in considerable numbers, to a range of standard patterns. However, there are many variations, and lesser makers often produced very individualistic pieces.

The dial is almost always brass, and really consists only of the chapter ring, as the dial centre is usually cut out. The more complex clocks have an elaborately pierced and scalloped dial. The earliest examples are engraved and silvered. On later versions, numerals are often painted on silvered brass (rather than engraved). Very late English skeletons have a painted dial. Some clocks have additional features such as a seconds dial and calendar dials. Hands are blued steel – brass hands would be difficult to read.

The earliest English skeleton clocks are timepieces only, and do not strike the hours. However, whether they are timepieces or striking clocks, the basic mechanism of the skeleton clock followed that of a bracket clock. As in bracket clocks, the only steel parts to the movement are the pinions and arbors; the rest of the mechanism is made of brass. Because they were designed for display, the movements are of the highest quality, and often show considerable technical ingenuity. All examples are spring-driven, with a fusee movement or a going barrel (see p.11). If a striking clock, there will be two trains (one for timekeeping, the other for striking). Skeleton clocks usually have an anchor escapement, although the most complex examples often have a balance wheel (see p.10).

English skeletons which strike the hours tend to do so on a gong. The gong was usually mounted behind the clock, although on examples by Samuel Condliff of Liverpool, the gong is inside the hollow base. Some skeletons simply strike the hours. Others strike the quarter-hours as well. Late 19thC examples may have elaborate striking work.

French skeletons were never produced on the same scale as in England. They are more restrained in design than English examples, and the more complex pieces typically incorporate mechanical refinements such as a compensated pendulum or subsidiary dials, rather than elaborately cut-out plates. French skeletons may have an anchor escapement, or else a pin wheel escapement (see p.10), a mechanism common to many French clocks from the late 18thC onward. Instead of a fusee movement, French skeletons are more likely to have a going barrel (see p.11). Dials are usually white enamel, with the centre cut out. There is always a glass dome to keep dust out, but French examples sometimes have a detachable wooden base, as well as a plinth – usually marble – to which the clock is fixed.

In spite of the great variety of skeletons produced, few of the more complex clocks come on the market today. The most desirable examples available are either timepieces or striking clocks by Samuel Condliff, as well as some of the more complicated French skeletons. However there are also many mid-19thC timepieces in circulation, usually with an anchor escapement and an inexpensive ebonized wood base.

An English skeleton timepiece by an unknown maker c.1845; ht 10in/25.5cm; value code F/G

Identification checklist for skeleton timepieces
1. Are the cut-out plates made entirely of brass?
2. On the more decorative timepieces, is the chapter ring elaborately cut out? (see pp.122-3)
3. Is there an oval base, made either of wood or marble?
4. Is the glass dome original? (see right)
5. Does the glass dome sit on a simple step on the base?
6. Is the clock spring-driven?
7. Is the spring in a capped drum?
8. Is there a fusee? (some clocks have a going barrel)
9. Are the hands blued steel?
10. Does the signature appear on an applied plaque?

Simple skeleton timepieces
In England, skeleton clocks were made from c.1830, although they were being made in France as early as c.1800 (see pp.128-9).

English skeleton timepieces (which tell the time but do not strike) consist of two types: simple, like the clocks shown on these two pages, and decorative

(see pp.122-3). Simple timepieces are made almost entirely of brass, with only the arbors, pinions and hands made of steel. The plates may be simple or extremely elaborate. Timepieces are common; late 19thC pieces are not as well proportioned as earlier ones.
* All skeleton clocks originally had a fitted glass dome; these are often broken or lost. On simple timepieces, the glass dome sits on a step in the base, so replacements are easier to find. For the purposes of photography, skeletons are often shown without their domes.
* There are a few fake timepieces and striking clocks. The plates lack the sharp edges typical of authentic pieces. Bases are likely to be ebonized.

Signatures
Most examples are signed by the maker, others by a retailer. Some inexpensive timepieces are unsigned, as are, surprisingly, some from the top of the market.
* The signature may be on a plaque on the base or movement.

Movements
Timepieces are spring-driven, with a fusee movement (see p.11). The spring is in a drum below the dial. Most are of eight-day duration. There are a few of longer duration.

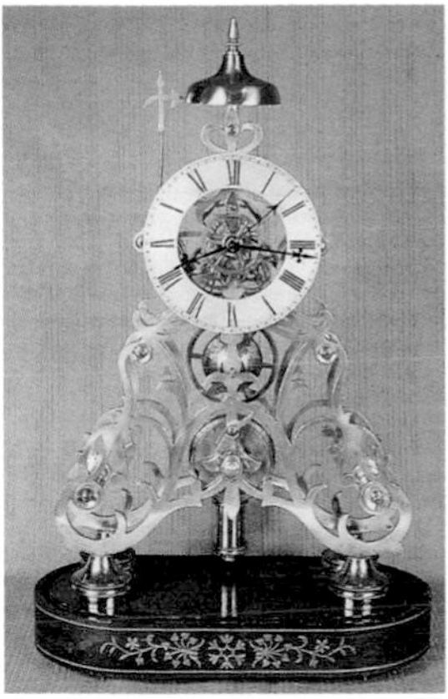

Most timepieces have an anchor escapement with a short pendulum, as on the c.1870 clock *above*. Unusually, the plates of this clock are silvered. There are a number of timepieces with a platform lever escapement, and no pendulum (see p.10). On the clock in the main picture, the balance mechanism is visible above the scalloped chapter ring.

Bases
The less expensive timepieces commonly have a base of ebonized wood. The base of a higher quality clock may be marble, or else veneered with mahogany, walnut or maple. Bases are usually oval, but some are rectangular. Decorative inlay on the base is a feature indicative of quality.
* The base may sit on bun feet.
* In the clock shown below left, the frame is attached to brass feet screwed to the top of the base.

The dial
The cut-out dial may be of white-painted brass with black-painted figures. The best dials are of silvered brass with black numerals. The shape of the hands varies, but they are usually blued steel, to show up against the brass background.

The shape of the dial ranges from a simple circular chapter ring with a cut-out centre, to more elaborate cut-out or scalloped chapter rings, as on the example *above*, made by Evans of Handsworth, c.1855, which features shaped edges and cut-outs between the figures.
* The Scott Memorial in Edinburgh, on which this piece was modelled, was a frequent subject. Architectural themes are common with complex skeleton clocks (see pp.126-7).

A decorative skeleton timepiece by James Condliff c.1855; ht 14in/35.5cm; value code D/E

Because of the many different types of decorative skeleton timepieces, it is not possible to provide a separate checklist. For a general checklist covering both simple and decorative skeleton timepieces, see p.120.

Decorative skeleton timepieces
Timepieces with more elaborate decoration occupied the higher end of the market during the first half of the 19thC. As with the simple timepieces, almost all of them are of eight-day duration with fusee movement and an anchor escapement (see p.10). The well proportioned timepiece in the main picture is signed by the retailer, Litherland, Davies and Co. of Liverpool, rather than the maker, James Condliff. Clocks signed by the retailer became increasingly common from the mid-19thC.

* The timepiece in the main picture has a going barrel (see p.11) instead of a fusee. The extremely large main wheel is intended simply to provide visual appeal.
* Although hands are usually made of blued steel, patterns vary widely. On this example, the simple pierced-tip hands suit the narrow silvered chapter ring.

Dials
Because the centre is almost always cut out, the dial of a skeleton clock really consists of just the chapter ring, which is almost always made of silvered brass. Decorative skeleton timepieces have a more ornate chapter ring than do the simple timepieces (see pp.120-1), and may be pierced or cut out.

Among the most famous producers of skeletons during the 19thC were John Pace and Benjamin Parker, of Bury St Edmunds. Pace was probably the retailer as well as the designer of decorative timepieces made by Parker, but they may be signed by either man (although always in the same hand). The use of Arabic numerals in a heavily fretted chapter ring, as on the c.1855 timepiece *above*, is peculiar to Pace and Parker.

The plates
The cut-out brass plates which make up the frame are attached by horizontal pillars secured with very fine blued steel screws.
* Decorative timepieces by W. F. Evans and Sons may be identified by their swirling "Arabesque" pattern plates.

Floral motifs, such as the "fuschia" pattern of the timepiece, *above*, were among the most popular frame designs.

Although this example, made by T. Morgan of Manchester c.1845, has a bell, it is not a true striking clock. Known as a "passing strike", the bell is struck once each hour.
* Most examples are signed by the maker. The clock shown below left is signed "T. Morgan" on the chapter ring below 12, with "Manchester" immediately opposite, above 6.

Bases
Marble bases – usually well-figured – are common on decorative timepieces. If the base is veneered, it is probably in mahogany, maple or rosewood. Ebonized wood was not usually used on such fine quality clocks.
* All examples have a glass dome.
* Some clocks are screwed to the base on conical or ball brass feet.

The tapered brass base of the unusual pyramidal timepiece with going barrel shown *above*, produced c.1855 by John Pace, is peculiar to Pace and Parker. Unusually, this example has a gilded – instead of the more usual silvered – chapter ring.
* Pace and Parker produced timepieces in a variety of durations, ranging from the basic eight-day, in the case of the example above, to as much as three months, or even one year.
* The feet on the base vary tremendously, but are usually ball- or bun-shaped.
* For fakes, see p.121.

A striking skeleton clock by J. Smith and Sons c.1850; ht 19½in/49.5cm; value code D/E

Identification checklist for striking skeleton clocks
1. Are the cut-out plates made entirely of brass?
2. Is there an oval base?
3. Is the glass dome original?
4. Is the dial silvered?
5. Are there two spring trains?
6. Do the wheels have 5 crossings, or spokes?
7. Does the signature appear on a plaque? (usually mounted on the frame)
8. Are the hands blued steel?

Striking skeleton clocks
In England, skeleton clocks that strike the hours began to appear in increasing numbers from the 1840s. Production continued until World War I. The basic frame is always brass. Like the simple timepieces, all striking skeletons are spring-driven, with a fusee movement and most commonly, an anchor escapement (see p.10). However, striking clocks have two spring trains – one train for going, and one for striking – and so appear quite different from the timepieces. Each train has a

fusee. Striking skeletons are usually of eight-day duration; it is rare to find any of longer duration. The wheels typically have five crossings (spokes): an invariable sign of quality.

* Wheels with six crossings were commonly used by W. F. Evans of Handsworth.

* Together with Evans, J. Smith and Sons of Clerkenwell produced more skeleton clocks than almost all the other makers combined. Skeletons by Smith often have a heavily fretted chapter ring.

Value point

A fitted glass dome is a very desirable feature, and indicative of high quality. If a dome has been lost, it can be very difficult to obtain a replacement.

The striking mechanism

Striking skeleton clocks strike the hours either on a coiled wire gong, or, less commonly, on a bell. They often repeat the hours when a cord attached to a lever on the movement is pulled. The gong is usually visible behind the movement. On the clock in the main picture, the conical gong stand is visible at the back of the base, to the right.

* The clock in the main picture also strikes once every half-hour on the bell above the frame.

In addition to striking the hours, the c.1860 clock, *above*, modelled on Lichfield Cathedral and made by Smith, also repeats the last hour struck. The repeat cord passes through a hole in the base to avoid the dome (not shown).

* Skeleton clocks were often modelled on famous buildings, and Lichfield Cathedral is a common motif. Others include Edinburgh's Scott Memorial (see p.121), the Brighton Pavilion, York Minster and St. Paul's Cathedral in London.

Identification

Most clocks are signed, the signature usually appearing on a plaque applied to the bottom of the plates rather than on the chapter ring.

* Although the clock in the main picture was made by Smith, it bears the plaque of a retailer, Brooking of Clifton, near Bristol. It can be identified as one from the Smith workshop because it resembles examples signed by that maker, or appearing in the firm's extant catalogues.

Dials are always silvered brass, Some are elaborately scalloped, or, like the clock shown *above*, pierced.

* Hands are invariably blued steel, in order to indicate the time clearly against the brass frame and movements. They can be quite complex in shape.

Bases

Bases are commonly marble or veneered wood. Hollow mahogany-veneered bases – often with a gong inside – are unique to James Condliff. The clock above is unusual in not being fixed to a base.

A three-train skeleton clock by J. Smith and Sons c.1870; ht 25½in/64.8cm; value code A

Identification checklist for complex skeleton clocks
1. Is the frame of the clock extremely elaborate?
2. Does the clock have an elaborate striking mechanism?
3. If visually simple, does it incorporate mechanical complications?
4. Does the clock have a fusee movement?
5. Does it have its original glass dome? (not always shown in photographs)
6. Does the clock have a signature? (perhaps on an applied plaque)

Complex skeleton clocks
Skeleton clocks with visually interesting or complex frames or movements, known as complex skeletons, were produced mainly from c.1860-80. All makers attempted to produce complex skeletons. The best are usually, but not always, signed. As they were the most expensive skeletons, few were produced. Their value ranges widely.

The frame
The brass frames of complex skeleton clocks are highly elaborate, and can look cluttered. The most elegant are usually the simplest, like the Condliff example, shown far right. As on the clock in the main picture, complex skeletons are often architectural in appearance. This clock was produced c.1860 by J. Smith and Sons of Clerkenwell,

and the elaborately pierced silvered dial is characteristic of this maker. The distinctive velvet-covered base indicates a clock of the highest quality.

Signatures
Skeleton clocks were often used as presentation pieces. The clock in the main picture, modelled on the Brighton Pavilion, bears the retailer's signature above the elaborate presentation plaque.

Condition
Because skeletons were made relatively recently and have usually been well cared for by owners, they tend to be in good condition today. Even on complex examples, replacement parts are seldom needed. Most pieces require only an occasional dusting. Cleaning should be done by an expert. The plates are polished and finished with a clear lacquer, which can be affected by contact with the hands. The brass should have an even, mellowed appearance.

Movements
Instead of an anchor escapement, complex skeletons often have a lever escapement (see p.10). All complex skeletons strike the hours. They frequently have three wheel trains instead of the more usual two. The third train enables them also to strike the quarter-hours.
* Some complex skeleton clocks feature subsidiary dials or musical work (see below).

Because it was fitted with a lever escapement, there is no pendulum on this ornate early clock, *above*, made by James Condliff c.1840.

* The enamel chapter ring of the clock below left is unusual.
* Fusee chains are usually of steel, although they may have been replaced by gut.

Backs
Although a skeleton clock was intended to be seen from the front, the back is generally well finished. Usually, a clock would be set up on a table or on a mantel. A mirror was sometimes placed behind those with very complex designs.

Fakes
It is very unlikely for a complex skeleton clock to have been faked. The amount of work involved means that it is not worthwhile. However, there are some fake timepieces and simple striking clocks (see p.120).

Although it has a complicated movement, the skeleton *above*, also produced by Condliff c.1860, has an uncluttered appearance. The hours and quarter-hours are struck on three coiled wire gongs concealed in the hollow base peculiar to this maker. The centre seconds hand is an uncommon feature.

Other complex skeletons
Variations include:
* Clocks which strike the hours on eight bells (with four trains)
* Musical clocks with 16 bells
* Table regulators: very accurate clocks, with a regulator dial and a compensated pendulum (see p.11), but a skeleton frame.

A French striking skeleton clock by Baltasar c.1800; ht 16in/41cm; value code C

Identification checklist for French skeleton clocks
1. Is the frame shaped like an upside-down letter Y?
2. Does the clock have a detachable wooden base?
3. Is the glass dome original?
4. Is there a white enamelled chapter ring?
5. Is the bezel engine-turned?
6. Are there any subsidiary dials?

French skeleton clocks
French skeleton clocks are more notable for mechanical refinements than for a flamboyant appearance. They were first produced in the late 18thC, but the majority date from c.1800-70. Most were made by Parisian makers, but never on the same scale as in England. Most are fairly simple in design, with the upside-down letter Y the most common form. Some are mechanically complex: the clock in the main picture has a gridiron pendulum (see p.117) for greater accuracy, a subsidiary dial for the date and day of the week and a centre seconds hand. A simple French skeleton would fetch much less than the complex one in the main picture. Both simple and complex examples are sought after today.

Dials
The dials of French skeleton clocks are almost always white enamel. Pierced chapter rings are unknown, but, as in the piece in the main picture, the dial centre may be cut out. The engine-turned brass bezel on the piece in the main picture is typical of a French skeleton.
* Hands are mainly blued steel; brass was occasionally used.

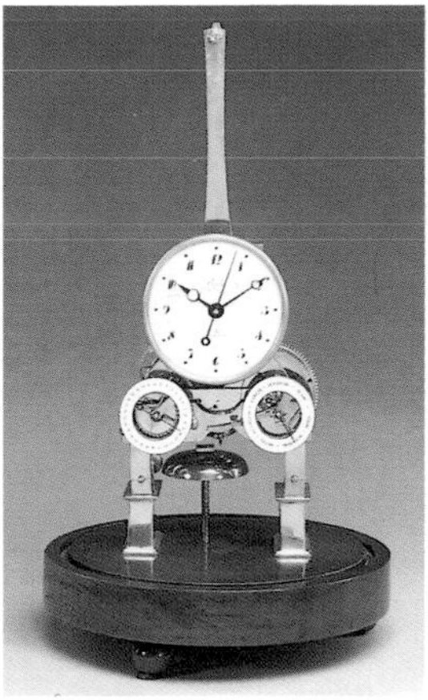

Subsidiary dials are common. The late 18thC clock *above*, made by Bouchet, shows the date and day of the week. The best clocks are signed on the dial by the maker, as here, or by a retailer.

Movements
Most French skeletons have a going barrel, and some have a fusee movement (see p.11). Most have either anchor or, as on the clock in the main picture, pin wheel escapement (see p.10). Most are of eight-day duration.

On the movement shown *above*, from the Bouchet clock, left, the pin wheel is just visible at the top. The bell on this clock is unusual: few French skeleton clocks strike the hours.

Bases
Unlike English skeletons, which are attached to a marble or wooden base, French ones have a marble plinth, which rests on a separate wooden base.

The marble plinth may feature applied and gilded metal mounts and mouldings, as on the early 19thC 12in/30cm-high timepiece with a fusee movement, shown *left*. Like English examples, all French skeleton clocks originally had a glass dome. The rare fitted glass dome of this clock has an unusual knobbed shape. It is uncommon to find a French skeleton clock that still has its original base and dome. Any clock that does is extremely desirable.

A carriage clock with grande *and* petite sonnerie
by Abraham-Louis Breguet c.1807

Carriage clocks are among the most extensively produced, most popular and most collected of all antique clocks. They are readily available, and represent the best investment – for a modest outlay – available on the market today.

These small, spring-driven shelf clocks could be carried easily – hence the name. They all have a top handle, and most French carriage clocks originally had a leather outer travelling case, also with a handle.

Carriage clocks were produced mainly during the 19thC, although there are many early 20thC examples. The vast majority were produced by French makers. The earliest true carriage clocks (their forerunner was the *pendule d'officier*, see p.81), were produced in Paris by Abraham-Louis Breguet at the beginning of the 19thC. By the 1870s, the manufacture of carriage clocks in France was a substantial industry. Separate craftsmen made the movements and the case: movements were often made in *Franche-Comté* or in

Normandy; the clock itself was assembled by a maker in Paris (or Geneva) who put his name on the dial and/or the movement. Leading makers included Breguet, Pierre Drocourt, Henri Jacot and François Margaine. All carriage clocks have a brass frame. On the earliest, the case was made of a single piece of cast brass. From c.1845, cases were more frequently assembled from many pieces. The size and decoration of the cases varies widely. However, French makers followed certain standard case shapes, of which the *Corniche* (Cornice) was the most common. Other common styles include the Gorge, or grooved case, and the Obis, or *Zèro bis* (''Double Zero''), the least expensive type of carriage case. Variations include oval cases, miniatures, and ''giant'' carriage clocks.

There are a huge number of decorative variations to the basic carriage clock design. Cases may be elaborately engraved. From c.1870, the most elaborate engraved cases feature enamel or – from c.1890 – porcelain panels in the sides and back of the case, as well as a decorated enamel dial. Engraved cases with decorative panels are among the most desirable of all carriage clocks.

Carriage clock dials are almost invariably white enamel, with black numerals and signature (if signed). The best quality examples have a brass mask fitted around the dial centre, usually featuring engraving or engine-turning.

Carriage clocks have a platform lever escapement (see p.10). Virtually all are of eight-day duration, with the going barrel (see p.11) common to French clocks. They vary from simple timepieces to complicated clocks with *grande sonnerie* striking (see p.12). Most strike on a gong; those with a bell are very sought after. Many striking clocks have a repeat button on the top of the case. When the button is pressed, the clock repeats the last hour struck (and possibly the last quarter-hour). Additional features include alarm, calendar dials and complex escape mechanisms.

English carriage clocks were produced in relatively small numbers, but generally by the best London makers. Cases are plainer than French carriages, but are more solid in appearance. They are spring-driven, and usually have a fine-quality fusee movement (see p.11). The best examples may have a chronometer escapement (see p.10), a very accurate mechanism used in marine chronometers. Some still have their substantial wooden travelling case.

All carriage clocks have a serial number, either on the dial or stamped on the movement. Where maker's records are available, the serial number can be a useful means of determining the date of manufacture. Each of the main French makers also had a mark, which was generally stamped on to the clock movement. If an English name appears on the dial of a clock with a French maker's mark, it is certain to be that of the person who sold it. However, the finest French carriage clocks may have no maker's mark visible at all, as the retailer who commissioned the clock may have wanted only his name to appear.

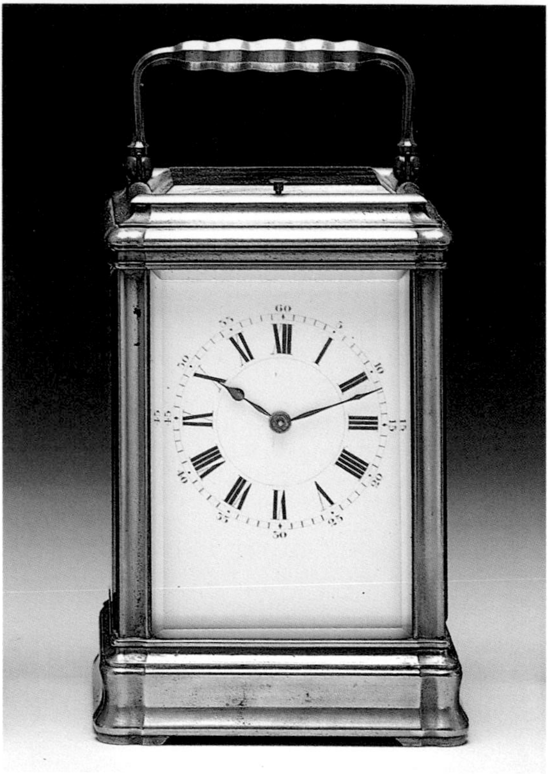

A plain-case carriage clock by Henri Jacot c.1890 ht 7in/17cm; value code F

Identification checklist for plain-case carriage clocks
1. Is the case brass, with no added ornament?
2. Is the dial enamelled?
3. Does the clock have a carrying handle?
4. Are there bevelled glass panels on the sides, back, front and top of the case?
5. Is there a repeat button in the centre front of the case top? (although a few do not repeat)
6. Does the piece have a serial number?
7. Is it signed? (either by the maker or a retailer)
8. Are the hands blued steel?

Plain-case carriage clocks
Carriage clocks with a plain brass case were made in France from the early 19thC until well into the 20thC. They were widely exported, especially to England. There are large numbers on the market. Most have an enamel dial, which may be set in an engraved or engine-turned mask.

* Replicas are still made, but are not intended to deceive. They can be identified by their platform escapement (see p.10), which is not as finely made as on original pieces. They may be signed in a 20thC style.
* Most French carriages had a leather carrying case. Few have their original case; surviving cases are often damaged.
* All carriages have a serial number, which appears on the backplate underneath the carrying case, and on the winding key: check that the numbers match. The key is often missing: any carriage clock with original case and key is a rarity.

Movements
Carriage clocks are spring-driven, with a going barrel (see p.11), and are of eight-day duration. If striking, it will do so on a gong, or, more rarely, on a bell.

Plain-cases with complex striking, as in the c.1840 example, *above*, by Louis Breguet, have a repeat button on the top of the case. When pushed, this repeats the last hour struck. This clock also has separate alarm and date dials. A single subsidiary dial (for alarm) is more common.
* The dial may be signed by an English retailer. Look for a maker's mark on the backplate (see right).

Cases
Plain-case carriage clocks always have a brass frame, which may be either polished and finished with clear lacquer, or else gilded. The brass frame is glazed on the front, sides and on the back door, and also on top. The "Gorge" case, like that in the main picture was used by the best makers for the more expensive clocks.

The *Corniche* (Cornice) case, like that of the example shown *above*, made by Jacot c.1890, was produced mainly in the late 19thC. These clocks may have elaborate striking; this one strikes the hours and half-hours, with a repeat button.
* Carrying handles vary in shape; on Jacot's Gorge-case clocks, the handle is straight-sided.
* Hands are usually blued steel. The chief makers had their own style. Drocourt favoured the "moon" pattern, *below left*, whereas Jacot used spade hands, *below right*. The trefoil hands, *below centre*, were used less often, and by various makers.

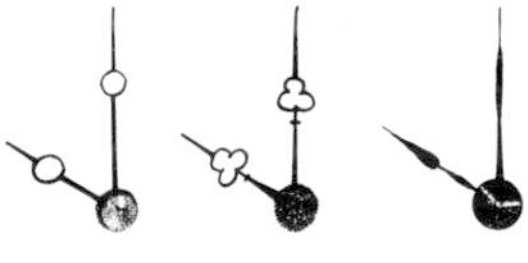

Marks
It is rare to find the full signature of the maker. Instead, carriage clocks may be identified by case style, or by reference to the stamped mark used by the major makers (see pp.178-83). The mark is nearly always found on the backplate.

A carriage clock with an engraved Gorge case, probably by Henri Jacot c.1870; ht 7in/18cm; value code E/F

Identification checklist for engraved-case carriage clocks
1. Is the case made entirely of brass?
2. Does the engraved decoration cover the whole surface of both case and handle?
3. Is the dial enamelled?
4. Does the clock have a striking mechanism?
5. Is there a repeat button?
6. Are the glass panels bevelled at the edges?
7. Does the piece have a serial number?
8. Are the hands blued steel?

Engraved-case carriage clocks
In most respects, carriage clocks featuring engraved decoration are identical to those with plain cases. As in the engraved Gorge case in the main picture, the engraving is mainly foliate or floral, and typically covers the whole surface of the brass case, as well as the carrying handle. The best engraving is dense and finely detailed, with smooth, elegant lines. It should cover as much of the case as possible. Dials are enamel, with blued steel hands. Engraved cases are more desirable and more expensive than plain cases.

* The signature on the dial is most commonly that of a London retailer. Unusually, the piece in the main picture bears the name of a French retailer, Rossel et Fils, who took over the firm of J.F. Bautte et Cie of Paris and Geneva. However, the movements may have been made by Jacot; look for a maker's mark inside the case. The French days of the week indicate that the clock was not for export.

The finest engraved cases have a brass mask around the dial itself. This may be engraved or else have engine-turning. Produced c.1840 by Paul Garnier – an important early carriage clock maker – this example, *above*, is typical of the one-piece style: the case was cast as a single piece and then fitted to its base.
* Carriage clocks are usually wound on the backplate. On the finest engraved cases, the back door is engraved, in place of the more usual glazing. Engraved backs have a shutter over the winding hole to keep dust out.

Movements
The movements of engraved-case carriage clocks are almost identical to those of plain cases (see pp.132-3). However, most engraved-case clocks strike the hours – usually on a gong but occasionally on a bell – and also have repeating work. Some have elaborate striking: the clock in the main picture has *grande sonnerie* striking on two bells, with repeat.

* Most examples have a repeat button, located on the top of the case. When pressed, the clock will repeat the last hour (or hour and quarter-hour) struck.

Oval cases, like that *above*, made c.1870 by J. Soldano, may strike on a bell instead of a gong. The curved glass on these rare clocks can be difficult to replace.

Subsidiary dials
Carriage clocks may have one or more subsidiary dials. These do not necessarily indicate high quality but are desirable features.

The most common subsidiary dial is an alarm, as on the fine Gorge case example *above*, signed by J. Klaftenberger of Regent Street. A subsidiary seconds dial on the main dial, as on the clock in the main picture, is very rare in a carriage clock.

An engraved-case carriage clock by Drocourt, with cloisonné panels c.1870; ht 7in/18cm; value code D/E

Identification checklist for porcelain and *cloisonné* panelled carriage clocks

1. Are the frame and handle made of brass?

2. If there are porcelain panels, do these show pastoral scenes?

3. Do *cloisonné* panels depict patterns of abstract or stylized foliage?

4. Is there a bevelled glass panel over the dial panel itself? (and also, on top of the case)

5. Are side panels decorated instead of glazed?

6. Does the piece have a serial number?

Panelled carriage clocks
Carriage clocks with decorative panels were produced in the last quarter of the 19thC, but never in large numbers. They rarely come up at auction today. The most common types of panelling are either porcelain, or *cloisonné* enamel (enamel fired into separate compartments and

divided by thin metal strips or wires). Usually, both dial and side panels will be decorated. The best examples also have a panelled back (and possibly a panelled top, as well). A bevelled glass panel covers the dial. The sides are unglazed.

* The frame is brass, and may be engraved (see pp.134-5).

* If a side panel has been cracked, both side panels will probably have been removed and replaced by bevelled glass.

Enamel cases

Cloisonné panels show stylized patterns of flowers or foliage. The clock in the main picture is typical.

* Limoges enamel was used, as well as *guilloche* – coloured translucent enamel fired over engraved or engine-turned metal.

The dial centre is usually plain, although on the example with a gilded brass dial, *above*, made by Richard et Cie c.1880, the *cloisonné* decoration covers the dial centre, as well as the base and handle.

Porcelain panelled cases

On carriage clocks with porcelain panels, the panels usually depict Italianate or pastoral scenes. Like enamelled cases, porcelain panelled examples were expensive. Few were made, but a number were produced for the Chinese market. The best are signed on the back panel.

Panelled cases are noted for visual appeal rather than complex movements. The c.1860 Gorge case *above* simply strikes the hours and half-hours.

"Giant" carriage clocks

The largest carriage clock, the "giant", averaged 9in/23cm in height. Few were produced, and only a few of these are panelled.

Subsidiary dials are rare on panelled clocks, as they break up the design. Some examples, like the finely engraved and panelled giant Gorge case *above*, made by Drocourt c.1870, may have an alarm. The Gorge case is the most common style of giant case.

A miniature carriage timepiece in an ebony and brass case c.1890; ht 4in/10cm; value code F

Identification checklist for miniature carriage clocks

1. Is the basic frame of the clock made of brass?
2. Is it a timepiece rather than a striking clock?
3. Does the case have quite a simple carrying handle?
4. Is the dial porcelain or enamelled?
5. Is there a serial number?
6. Are the hands blued steel?

Miniature carriage clocks
Miniature carriage clocks, also known as *mignonettes*, or "little darlings", were produced mainly during the late 19thC. They were made by French makers, but not in large numbers. Miniatures are more sought after today than examples of standard size.

Cases
The cases of miniature carriage clocks vary widely, both in shape and materials. All examples have a brass frame with a carrying handle. The use of ebony on the frame of the timepiece in the main picture is unusual in a carriage clock.

Decoration could be as elaborate as on standard-size carriage clocks. The 3¼in/8.2cm porcelain panelled miniature timepiece *above*, produced c.1890, is typical.

* Miniatures were also produced with *cloisonné* panels and engraved cases.
* All have a serial number.

Size

Miniatures are of three standard sizes. *Mignonette No.1* stands only 1¾in/4.4cm in height (with the handle up). *Mignonette Nos.2* and *3*, were 4in/10cm and 4¼in/10.8cm in height, respectively. However, sizes of miniatures also varied according to the maker's taste.

This tiny silver gilt and enamel miniature *above*, produced c.1915, is only 1¾in/4.4cm in height. Cases of this size are unlikely to be fully engraved. As on this example, the handles of miniature carriage clocks are simpler in design than the standard size carriage clock.

Movements

Miniatures are nearly always timepieces rather than striking clocks: their small size made it impractical to fit a standard striking movement of eight-day duration. Most have a platform lever escapement (see p.10), although cylinder escapements (see p.10) are also found. Movements are always the same size, even if the case size varies.

* Some examples have alarm, striking or repeat work.

Condition

The only part of a carriage clock that may need to be replaced is the platform. Although modern replacements function perfectly, they appear cruder, and so detract substantially from value.

Signatures

Many miniatures are unsigned: the dials are too small for a signature and even the backplate is often not signed.

The *Obis* was the most inexpensive and most popular case style for standard size carriage clocks. Unusually, the dial on this 2½in/6.3cm *Obis*-style miniature timepiece, *above*, is signed and marked with the eagle of the seller, Henry Capt.

* Dials are usually enamelled. A damaged dial should be avoided. Anything more than hairline cracking is unlikely to be acceptable.

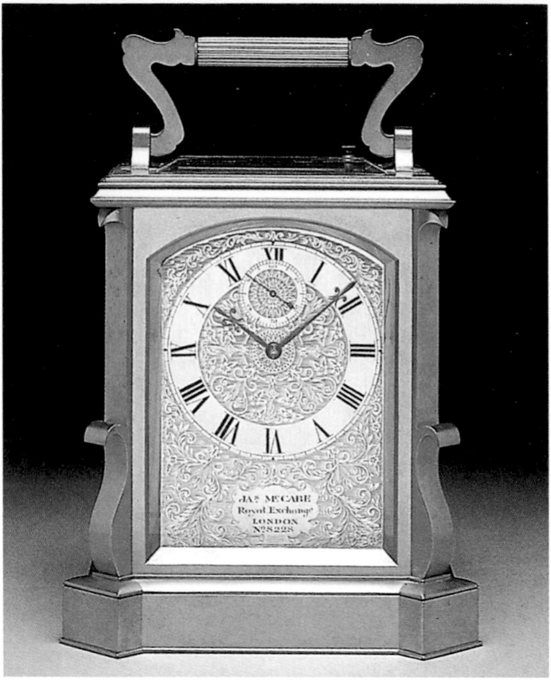

An English carriage clock by James McCabe c.1860; 9¾in/25cm; value code C/D

Identification checklist for English carriage clocks
1. Is the clock relatively simple in appearance?
2. Does it have a carrying handle?
3. Is the case made of gilded brass? (or, rarely, bronze)
4. Is there an engraved silvered dial? (some are gilded)
5. Is there a serial number?
6. Does the clock have a fusee movement?
7. Is the clock signed on the dial and on the backplate?
8. Are the hands blued steel?

English carriage clocks
Although produced in far smaller numbers than French carriage clocks, English carriage clocks were made to the highest standards. Most were made by London firms, although Liverpool makers also produced significant numbers. Their high value today reflects their scarcity, as well as the high quality of their movements. Like the clock in the main picture, the cases of English carriage clocks are almost always gilded brass, although a few are bronze-cased. Cases tend to be simple, even slightly severe in appearance, and are rarely engraved.
* The sides and back are usually glazed, but the back door is sometimes solid. The clock is wound from the back through shuttered holes.
* The case may have shallow pad or bun feet, or no feet at all.

* Hands are almost always blued steel. Those tipped by small *fleurs-de-lys* are characteristic of the McCabe firm, and were also used on their chronometers.

The dial
Like that of the clock in the main picture, the dials of English carriage clocks are typically engraved and silvered. As with French carriage clocks, nearly all have a serial number, frequently on the dial, and nearly always on the backplate.

Except for a seconds dial, subsidiary dials are unusual on English carriage clocks. However, the example *above* features an up/down dial, a device used to indicate the state of winding (see p.147). The up/down dial is more common on marine chronometers. Some dials have a gilded mask, as this one does. This clock was produced c.1915 by Charles Frodsham.
* Unlike French carriage clocks, English examples are always signed by the maker, usually on both the dial and backplate.

Movements
English carriage clocks are all spring-driven with a platform lever escapement (see p.10), and are of eight-day duration. They have a fusee movement (see p.11) instead of a going barrel. Most strike the hours, although there are some timepieces. Striking clocks usually repeat the hours automatically when a button on top of the case is pushed, and strike on a gong.

A feature of English carriage clocks, like the bronze-cased example *above*, made by James McCabe, c.1860, is a small spring which continues to supply power to the train during winding. This device, known as maintaining power, is common in very precise clocks such as regulators (see pp.110-17).
* Some English carriages still have their original mahogany travelling case. The case is usually signed, and should have the serial number of the clock.

Unusually, this early English carriage clock, *above*, produced c.1835 by the famed London firm of Vulliamy, is signed on the chapter ring, at the top. This example is also uncommon in being wound from the front.

STRUT CLOCKS

A strut calendar timepiece attributed to Thomas Cole c.1854; ht 6in/15cm; value code F

Identification checklist for strut clocks
1. Is the case brass, with fine engraving and chasing?
2. Does the clock stand upright at a slight angle, by means of a folding strut (undecorated) mounted on the backplate or a swivelling foot (usually engraved)?
3. Is there a loop on the top of the case?
4. Does the clock have an engraved and silvered dial?
5. Are there any subsidiary or calendar dials?
6. Are the hands blued steel, perhaps with a *fleur-de-lys* motif on the tips?
7. Is the clock signed?

Strut clocks
A distinctive variation on the carriage clock is the strut clock, which takes its name from the folding brass strut mounted on the backplate. When extended, the strut holds the clock upright at a slight angle. In addition to a strut, many have a swivelling foot mounted on the bottom of the case. From the number that still have their original leather travelling cases, they were probably designed to be used as travelling clocks. Strut clocks average ¾-1in/1.9-2.5cm in thickness. When stood upright on a table, they resemble a picture in a frame. They are sought-after today, but do not come up as regularly at auction as some other clocks.

Thomas Cole
Strut clocks were produced c.1825-65. Virtually all were made by the London maker Thomas Cole (1800-64), who specialized in ornamental timepieces and novelty clocks (see p.164). Cole made around 1,600 strut clocks, of which 1,400 are numbered.
* There are a few imitations of Cole strut clocks, made at the same time as his, on the market. The quality of the engraving may vary, but some are the equal of Cole's own work.

Signatures
Cole signed many clocks; the stamped signature (and number) is inside the case. but often in a very inaccessible place. However, the signature on the dial is typically that of the London retailer. The clock in the main picture is signed "J.F. Hancock" of Bruton Street.

THOS COLE
LONDON

Movements
Strut clocks are all spring-driven, but with a going barrel (see p.11) rather than a fusee movement. Almost all are timepieces, although a few strike the hours. Like most carriage clocks, all strut clocks have a platform lever escapement (see p.10). However, in order to fit the movement into the slim case, the escapement is mounted vertically rather than horizontally (as in carriage clocks). Many strut clocks are of 30-hour duration, but those in larger and more expensive cases are usually of eight-day duration.

The case
The case is made of engraved and chased brass, and is frequently gilded. On the best quality strut clocks, the engraving is extremely intricate and more finely and deeply cut than on less expensive pieces or imitations. The rectangular case with rounded corners, like that in the main picture, is the most typical shape. The case consists of up to 10 layers of cast brass sections which are then screwed together.
* The top tag, which allows the clock to be hung on a wall, is a typical feature.

Case variations include the diamond, the octagon or, as on the c.1850 gilt brass timepiece shown *above*, the oval.
* The back (and strut) is not engraved, but may be gilded.

The dial
Most dials are silvered brass, and usually have very fine engraving, with numerals and subsidiary indications in black. The engraving on the dial is always of equal quality to that on the case. There are a few gilded dials.

Subsidiary dials are common. The c.1900 clock *above* shows the day and the month. Calendars are also common.
* Hands are blued steel. The tips often have a *fleur-de-lys* motif.

Condition
Movements easily break if the clock is dropped. They should be regularly overhauled.

MARINE CHRONOMETERS

A marine chronometer of eight-day duration by John Arnold, c.1804

Marine chronometers are very accurate spring-driven clocks developed for use at sea. These precision timekeepers – halfway between a scientific instrument and a clock – provided mariners with accurate timekeeping, enabling them to determine exact longitude.

In 1714, the British Parliament offered prizes of £10,000, £15,000 and £20,000 for the discovery of a method of determining longitude within 60, 40 or 30 miles. In 1735, the Yorkshire maker John Harrison produced the first of a series of accurate timepieces which overcame the effects of both temperature changes and of the motion of the ship. In 1763, Harrison claimed the prize of £20,000. His invention showed the exact time at Greenwich, to the nearest second, permitting mariners to determine their position by reference to astronomical data contained in the Nautical Almanac. With the growth of trade and empire, the demand for chronometers grew rapidly. By the 19thC, they were standard equipment on all British merchant or naval ships over a certain tonnage. Chronometers were also produced on the Continent of Europe and in the United States.

The chronometer was always mounted horizontally on gimbals (rotating brackets) in the bottom section of a three-section wooden box. The hinged middle section opens, but is glazed on top to protect the chronometer from dust and moisture. The top section, or lid is also hinged (but has often been removed or lost). Cases are generally mahogany, but there are some examples – possibly produced for large yachts – in rosewood or coromandel. These cases may also have brass stringing or a finely shaped brass escutcheon.

The dials of most marine chronometers are engraved and silvered brass. Very early French, and some early English examples have an enamel dial. Almost all have blued steel hands, although some are gold. Hands are usually simple in shape, with a spade motif on the tips.

All marine chronometers are spring-driven, and have a sophisticated form of escapement known as a chronometer escapement. This was a variation on the lever escapement (see p.10). Over the years, individual makers made various improvements to the mechanism, in order to compensate for changes in temperature. Any refinements to the escape mechanism increase the value of the clock. The movements of chronometers are always finely made and often fascinating to look at. To inspect the mechanism, the chronometer must be removed from the brass bowl in which it is housed. All examples should have their original winding key, which may bear the instrument's serial number.

All chronometers were numbered and signed by the maker. However, the signature on the dial may be that of the ship's chandler (outfitter) or agent who sold the chronometer. Each chronometer features an "ivory" – a small plaque recessed into the centre section of the case – which shows the maker's name (and possibly his address) and the serial number of the chronometer. Originally, all these plaques were ivory, hence the name. However, some are made from mother-of-pearl, and there are recent replacements made from plastic.

Marine chronometers are fascinating to collect, especially if the marine history of a particular example is known. A number of English makers, such as Barraud, Frodsham and Dent specialized in the production of these pieces, in addition to their output of standard domestic clocks.

The value of any marine chronometer depends on its age, duration, condition, the maker's importance and any specific technical refinements. There are a fairly large number in circulation today, and they can be relatively inexpensive to purchase. English chronometers are considered the most collectable, but very early French examples – by such makers as Breguet, Berthoud and Motel – also command substantial prices. Pieces are usually in good condition, as they were generally well cared for. As long as it is regularly overhauled, any chronometer will keep very good time.

MARINE CHRONOMETERS: 1

A marine chronometer of two-day duration by Charles Frodsham c.1880; diameter 4¾in/12cm; value code F

Identification checklist for English marine chronometers
1. Is the chronometer mounted in gimbals (pivoted rings) in a three-section wooden case?
2. Is the case mahogany? (coromandel is uncommon)
3. Is there an engraved and silvered brass dial?
4. Is there a subsidiary up/down dial? (see below)
5. Is there a subsidiary seconds dial?
6. Does the case have an applied plaque (perhaps ivory) with the maker's name and the number of the clock?
7. Are there any carrying handles?
8. Does the chronometer have its original winding key?
9. Is it signed on the dial?

Early English marine chronometers
The earliest English marine chronometers were of one-day duration. Most were made from c.1810, but are very rare today. More common are those of two-day duration, like the example in the main picture. Most chronometers on the market were made during the 19thC: 18thC examples are rare.

The case

Marine chronometers are always contained in a three-section box, commonly made of mahogany. On the chronometer in the main picture, the case is veneered with coromandel; a very unusual feature. This chronometer may have been produced for a large private yacht. Cases generally have carrying handles, which may be simple or fairly elaborate in shape. Examples produced for private yachts may be highly decorative. The chronometer was housed in the bottom section, and was hung in brass gimbals (pivoted rings) to keep it horizontal. The gimbals also allow the chronometer to be turned over to be wound.

As on the two-day example shown *above*, a hinged centre section, glazed on top, covers the chronometer, while a lid covers the glazed top. This piece was made c.1830 by Barraud and Sons.

* The top lid was often removed at sea, and may be missing today. Replacements often do not match the rest of the case.
* Hinges may be of the long "piano" type, with a brass stay, as on the example in the main picture, or else a pair of stopped hinges, as here, which keeps the lid open at about 90 degrees.

The dial

The glass-covered dial is nearly always silvered and engraved, with a subsidiary seconds dial and blued steel hands.

* All dials are signed, either by the maker or by a retailer.
* The gimbal lock at the lower right corner holds the gimbals when the chronometer is moved. It is found on all examples.
* The winding key is always housed in the corner of the case.
* The up/down dial just above the dial centre, is universal to marine chronometers, and shows how much time the clock has left to run. On two-day examples, the up/down dial runs from 0 to 56. On eight-day chronometers (see pp.148-9), the dial runs from 0 to 8 (indicating days).

The "ivory"

All chronometers originally had an "ivory" – a round plaque with the maker's name and the serial number of the clock – set into the case. Originally, most were actually ivory, but there were a few in brass. On the example in the main picture, the "ivory" is mother-of pearl; a feature indicative of high quality.

* The "ivory" has often been lost. In recent years, plastic replacements have appeared.

Movements

All chronometers are spring-driven timepieces with a fusee movement (see p.11) and a chronometer escapement (see p.10), which was a particularly accurate mechanism.

The two-day chronometer movement *above*, made by the London makers Parkinson and Frodsham c.1840, shows the balance and the single winding arbor.

* The back of the chronometer is usually housed in a brass bowl.
* It is unusual to find the maker's signature on the movement of a two-day chronometer, although it is typical of some examples by Charles Frodsham and the firm of Parkinson and Frodsham.

MARINE CHRONOMETERS: 2

Eight-day marine chronometers
Like chronometers of two-day duration, those of eight-day duration were produced throughout the 19thC, and until the end of World War II.

The two types appear the same, but the main visual difference lies in the subsidiary up/down dial, above the dial centre, which indicates how much time the clock has left to run. As on the chronometer *above*, produced by Victor Kullberg, the up/down dial on an eight-day example runs from 0 to 8 (indicating days) instead of from 0 to 56 (indicating hours).
* The silvered sight ring around the dial is common to later examples with a flat glass cover.
* Most eight-day chronometers were produced by London makers, although a few were made in Liverpool and some Scottish ports. Some bear the name of a foreign retailer. English pieces always have a fusee (see p.11).

The movement of this eight-day chronometer, *above*, produced by Kullberg and dated 1919, is more complex than that found on a two-day piece. The backplates are cut away to receive the escapement, which is mounted within separate plates.

Value point
The distinctive chequered pattern visible on the plates of the movement above is known as "spotting". This type of machine-engraved decoration is quite common on both two- and eight-day pieces. Spotting is a desirable feature, but can disappear if the movement is buffed or polished too hard.

The broad arrow mark shown *above*, is engraved on the backplate of the Kullberg movement shown below left, and indicates that the clock was made for the British Admiralty. The mark does not affect value.

The top lid was often removed so the dial could be visible at all times. As on the eight-day example *above*, made by R.M. Hunter and Co, a glass panel protected the clock. The lid has often been lost, which substantially reduces value.

Condition
On elaborate cases, damp may cause veneers or stringing to lift.
* The "ivory" should be original and match the signature and serial number on the dial.

Collecting
Chronometers of eight-day duration are much less common than those of two-day duration, and so are more valuable today. However, both kinds are still relatively inexpensive.
* English chronometers are the most sought-after, but early French examples (see pp.150-1) also command high prices.

Signatures
In the late 19thC, it was not unusual for the ivory, (and even the dial) to bear the name of a retailer, or of a ship's chandler or outfitter. However, the dial is usually also signed by the maker.

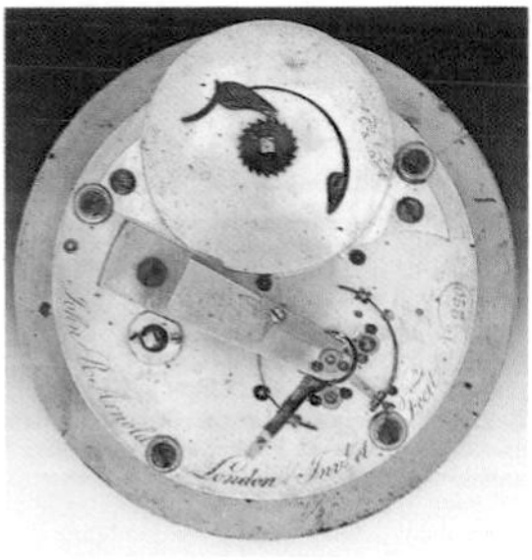

In addition to the dial, marine chronometers of eight-day duration are usually also signed on the movement. The movement shown *above*, from an eight-day chronometer produced c.1804 by the London maker John Arnold, is typical, and also shows the serial number below the Z-shaped balance.

The enamel dial shown *left*, from the Arnold chronometer shown above, is a very unusual feature. Dials are usually made of engraved and silvered brass. Also shown is the original winding key: a very desirable feature. An original key may be engraved with the same serial number as the dial and the ivory.

Ship's clocks
Unlike marine chronometers, ship's clocks were made in a round brass case to be screwed onto a bulkhead. Dials are usually silvered brass or enamelled metal, although some later examples are painted metal. Although produced in England from c.1860 until World War II, it is the rare early examples with a fusee movement (see p.11) that are the most collectable today. Later pieces, with a going barrel (see p.11), are less sought after. All have a seconds dial, blued steel hands (some are brass) and a signature on the dial.
* Almost all are timepieces only. Ship's clocks which strike the hours are rare, as are those that strike on two bells for watches.
* Unlike chronometers, not all have a serial number.

The up/down dial on the miniature *above*, made c.1875, is a nice refinement, and rare on a ship's clock. Although this example is signed by Simpson Benzie of Cowes, the majority of ship's clocks were produced by London firms.

Other marine chronometers
After c.1835, the basic design of the marine chronometer changed very little. Although English makers continued to produce the finest examples, makers on the Continent of Europe and, later, in the United States produced high quality instruments, often of distinctive appearance. In some cases, the movements of these were made in England and sold by a foreign retailer.
* Like English chronometers, those by Continental and American makers are spring-driven, with a chronometer escapement (see p.10). They are of two- or eight-day duration.
* For checklist, see p.146.

French chronometers
Marine chronometers were produced in France from the late 18thC. As a maritime power, France had the same need as England for an accurate marine timekeeper. Many French examples have a going barrel, instead of a fusee (see p.11). As on English examples, all are suspended in gimbals. Some leading makers include:
* Louis Berthoud
* Louis Leroy
* Jean François Henri Motel
* Abraham-Louis Breguet.

Most French chronometers have an enamel dial, instead of the engraved and silvered brass dial common on English examples. The chronometer shown *above*, is typical. It was produced c.1810 by Louis Berthoud. As with English examples, all French chronometers have a three-section wooden case. Cases are usually mahogany, which is durable and not subject to warping. There will often be a sliding panel in the top section – instead of an opening lid – to allow the dial to be seen.
* All French chronometers are numbered on the dial and usually on a brass plate fixed to the case.
* The label inside the case may be that of the chronometer adjuster, or the retailer. The label, which is found on some English chronometers, may state how much time the clock gains or loses (if any) during the week, or when it was last oiled.

The unusual marine chronometer shown *above*, was produced c.1815 by Abraham-Louis Breguet. Originally, it had a wooden case. However, in 1821 the clock was remounted in a rare silver *portique* (portico) case and adapted for display on a shelf or table. The unusual silvered brass dial shows hours on a subsidiary dial above the dial centre, with seconds shown on the lower subsidiary dial. The two winding holes do not indicate a striking clock: the clock has two going barrels, to maintain an even supply of power to the movement during winding.
* Breguet produced watches, table regulators and some of the first (and best quality) carriage clocks. He made many clocks in the *portique* style (also known as *pendule de voyage*), which was used by few other makers.

The green agate case on the chronometer *above* is extremely uncommon. The case was made by the jeweller Carl Fabergé, probably for use on a private yacht. The chronometer itself, which is of two-day duration, was produced by the Swiss firm of Ulysse Nardin, founded in 1846 and still in business.

The United States
The earliest American marine chronometer was patented in 1812 by William Bond of Boston, and significant numbers were produced by Bond and many other makers (see below) during the 19thC. Large numbers of marine chronometers were produced during World War II.
* Most cases are mahogany, although rosewood was used on some 19thC examples.
* American marine chronometers are sought-after in the United States and in Europe. Prices have risen in recent years.

Makers
Other important American makers include:
* John Bliss, New York
* Bliss and Creighton, Brooklyn
* T. S. and J.D. Negus, New York
* H. H. Heinrich, New York
* Elgin National Watch Co., Elgin, Illinois
* Hamilton Watch Co., Lancaster, Pennsylvania.

Hamilton marine chronometers
One of the best-known American chronometer makers is the Hamilton Watch Company, founded in 1892. From 1943, this firm produced more than 13,000 chronometers of two-day duration for the U.S. armed forces. The most common types are the Model 21 and the Model 22.
* All Hamilton chronometers are mounted in a mahogany case.

The dials of Hamilton marine chronometers, like the example *above*, from a Model 22, are of silvered brass and always have black Arabic numerals. The up/down dial above the dial centre shows how long the clock has left to run (see p.147). As this is a two-day clock, the dial runs from 0 to 56.

Hamilton movements are mass-produced, but are of high quality. The Model 21, as shown in the movement *above*, has a lever escapement (see p.10). The chain fusee movement (see p.11) is clearly visible on the right.
* The Model 22 also has a lever escapement, but has a going barrel instead of a fusee.

Replicas
A number of replica Model 21s were made during the 1980s. These should be avoided. Replicas can be identified by the Roman numerals on the dial.

Collecting
Because English chonometers were of very high quality, any foreign-made chronometers on the British market today are most likely to be early 19thC examples by the best French makers.

VIENNA REGULATORS

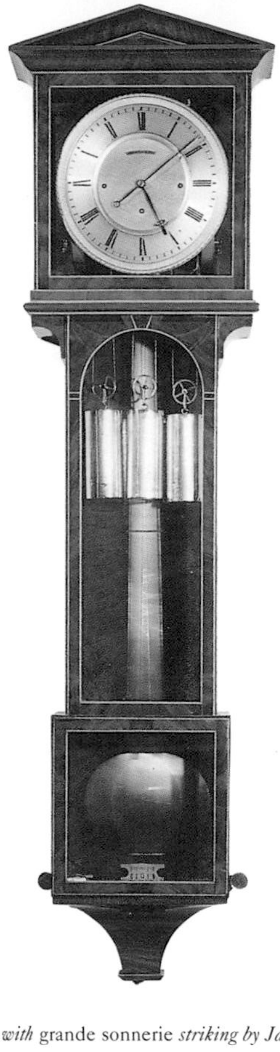

A Laterndluhr *with* grande sonnerie *striking by Jacob Zach, c.1820*

Vienna regulators are among the finest clocks ever produced. Although clockmaking in Austria dates back to the 16thC, the finest Viennese wall and longcase clocks were produced in the space of no more than 45 years, from c.1800 to c.1845. However, after 1845 the classic, restrained style of the Viennese case degenerated into the fussy and overdecorated cases of factory-made imitations produced mainly by German makers during the 1880s.

The term "Vienna regulator" usually refers to a weight-driven precision clock that is hung on a wall. There are two main types: the *Laterndluhr*, or lantern clock, has a large top and bottom, with a slimmer middle section; the *Dachluhr*, or rooftop clock typically features an architectural top and single-section case. All Vienna regulators have glazed door and side panels. Some remarkable examples of the floor-standing regulator were made, but these represent only a tiny proportion of Viennese production.

The refinement and delicate construction of the Viennese case was matched by that of both dial and movement. Whether the dial is enamel, silvered brass or the so-called milk glass, the numerals will invariably be finely written. Features such as bezels and even the dial centre may be engine-turned with the most intricate patterns. The floor-standing regulator will often have two or three subsidiary dials and be of long duration. Like all Vienna regulators, it is an extremely accurate timekeeper.

The compact movements are of light construction and contained in a very small space. Nearly all Vienna regulators are weight-driven, with a long pendulum, and usually, a dead beat escapement (see p.173). Some regulators have a seconds-beating pendulum, but the smaller Viennese wall-hanging regulators cannot accommodate a full-length seconds pendulum. Typically, where a seconds dial has been provided, the seconds hand takes only 45-55 seconds to complete a revolution, although this does not affect the accuracy of the minutes and hours. Because they are housed in larger cases, the Viennese floor-standing regulators are able to beat actual, or true seconds.

The most commonly employed case veneer is mahogany, often with thin, contrasting stringing in lighter woods, such as maple. Other veneers were sometimes used, particularly walnut, which was cut to produce a very effective figuring. Occasionally, ash was used, and its pale colour and pronounced figuring produced some of the most distinctive examples of the casemaker's art. There are also some cases veneered with ebonized wood (pale wood stained black).

Most Vienna regulators carry the signature of a maker in or around Vienna. Occasionally, a signature will be followed by "Pest" (indicating Budapest), or another city of the Austrian empire. It is not clear whether all such clocks were actually made in the city shown, or whether cases and/or movements were ordered from craftsmen in Vienna.

Because they were produced relatively recently, Vienna regulators are generally in good condition today. On examples with enamelled dials, there may be chips or cracks to the dial surface. However, some hairline cracks are usually considered to be acceptable. On regulators with a silvered dial, the figures and signature should appear crisp and unworn. In recent years, with the growing interest in Viennese clockmaking, the occasional fake or reproduction has appeared on the market.

The most collectable clocks today are timepieces of eight-day duration in a *Dachluhr* case. These were made in the largest numbers of any Vienna regulator of the period. They are slightly smaller than the *Laterndluhr*, and so are easier to house. The classic simplicity of the *Dachluhr* lends itself to almost any scheme of furnishing. They are still the most affordable of all the early Vienna regulators.

LATERNDLUHR

A mahogany Laterndluhr *by Johann Sachs c.1820; ht 40in/102cm; value code A*

Identification checklist for *Laterndluhr* regulators
1. Does the clock have an architectural top?
2. Does the hood slide off?
3. Do the centre and bottom sections lift out?
4. Is the case veneered with mahogany? (walnut is rare)
5. Is the inside of the case veneered?
6. Does the dial have either one winding hole (for a timepiece) or three (for a striking clock)?
7. Is the back only roughly finished?
8. Is the clock signed by the maker on the dial?
9. Are the hands of blued steel?

Laterndluhr
The *Laterndluhr*, or lantern clock, was first made c.1800. There were makers in other cities of the Austrian empire, but the best were Vienna-based and included:
* Joseph Jessner (1814-48)
* Philipp Fertbauer (1800-50)
* Anton Liszt (1828-58)

The case
Cases consist of three sections, each with glazed front and sides. The upper section has an architectural top. The glazed fronts of both lower sections may be lifted out, and are held in place by wooden lugs. Cases (including interiors) are mahogany-veneered. The sides are thin, but the back is thick enough to prevent the case from warping. Backs are plain, as all *Laterndluhr* are wall-hung.

Caution
The pendulum must be secured if the clock is moved, or else it may break one of the glass panels.

Unlike the clock in the main picture, which features a two-piece dial with an engine-turned centre, the early 19thC clock shown *above* has a one-piece silvered dial. Some examples have enamel dials. Hands are usually blued steel.

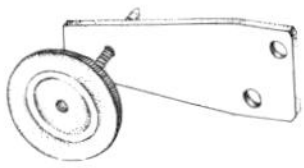

Most Vienna regulators feature two "steady" screws mounted on brass plates at the bottom of the case to help keep the clock stable. As shown *above*, the steady screw consists of a plate, which is fixed to the case, with a threaded screw running through it. The screw holds the clock in position against the wall.

Movements
Laterndluhr are weight-driven, with a pendulum and an anchor escapement (see p.10). Some are timepieces, others have *grande sonnerie* striking (see p.12). Because of the case length, the pendulum may not be long enough to beat true seconds. In this case, the seconds dial will revolve in 45-50 seconds. This does not affect accuracy.
* Most are of eight-day duration. Some are of one-, three- or six-month, or, rarely, year-duration.
* Beware of an original movement housed in a modern case.

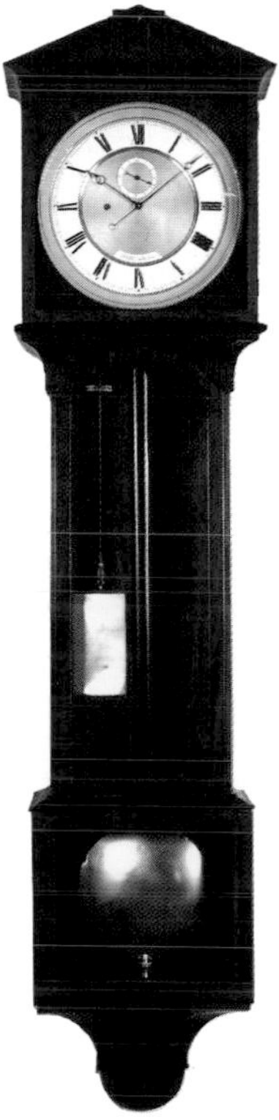

This rare early *Laterndluhr*, *above*, made c.1820, is of one-month duration. It also features a seconds dial and its large bob beats true seconds. The weight is positioned to one side in order to help the bob clear the weight. The small concave wooden mouldings below the hood are a common feature of *Laterndluhr*.

DACHLUHR

A Dachluhr *by Franz Schmidl*
c.1830; ht 37in/94cm; value code D

Identification checklist for Viennese rooftop regulators
1. Does the case have a simple architectural top?
2. Is it veneered with mahogany?
3. Is the case six-light? (i.e. with six glass panels)
4. Is the interior as well as the exterior of the case veneered?
5. Does the dial have one winding hole? (indicating a timepiece rather than a striking clock)
6. Does the piece have a full-length hinged door?
7. Are the hands of blued steel?
8. Is the dial signed by the maker?

Rooftop clocks
The *Dachluhr* (rooftop) case, with its characteristic simple architectural top and elegant lines, is roughly contemporary with the *Laterndluhr* (see pp.154-5), but was first produced c.1820. Like the classic rooftop in the main picture, the cases of these clocks are usually veneered with mahogany. The inside of the case is also veneered. Because these clocks are hung on the wall, the back was only roughly finished.
* The cases of rooftop clocks are known as "six-light", because they have six glazed sections. *Laterndluhr* have nine.
* The glass cover on the dials of Vienna regulators is usually of milk glass, a slightly opaque white glass made by adding tin or stannic oxide to the glass body. Milk glass was used throughout the 19thC. It tends to lack the crispness of modern glass.

Collecting point
Although the movements of both rooftop clocks and *Laterndluhr* are of the same high quality, rooftop clocks are more common than *Laterndluhr*, and so are generally less sought after.
* Most *Dachluhr* are of eight-day duration. Month-duration pieces are more desirable.

Some rooftop clocks have a one-piece enamel dial, as in the example shown *above*, made c.1830 by the firm of Elsner and Petrovits. Alternatively, they may have a one- or two-piece silvered dial. Most do not strike the hours: the single winding hole (and weight) on this clock indicates a timepiece.
* Some large rooftops have *grande sonnerie* striking (see p.12).
* Unusually, this case is walnut, not mahogany.

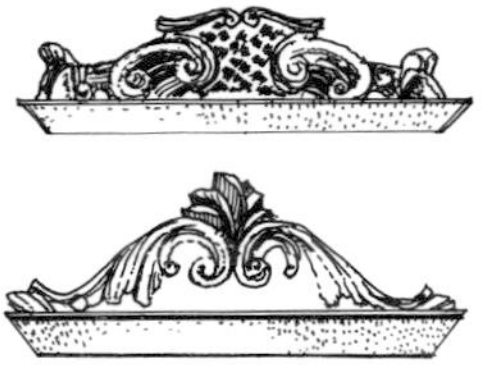

Some rooftop regulators may include elaborate carved cresting on the top of the case, as shown *above*. Such features may be found on timepieces and striking clocks.

As with the *Laterndluhr*, rooftop clocks used the range of standard Vienna hands, which were usually of blued steel. As in the dial shown *above*, produced c.1830 by Franz Schmidl, the long minute hand often features a counterpoise to balance the weight. This feature serves to reduce the strain on the movement when the minute hand is going "uphill".

The beat scale
Many rooftop clocks feature a beat scale, used to ensure that the arc of the pendulum is even. The pendulum should swing the same amount on either side of the centre of the scale. If the swing varies, the clock is not vertically aligned and the pallets (see p.10) are not engaging the escape wheel equally.

The beat scale may be screwed to the backboard, as shown in the detail *above*, or else secured to the floor of the case.

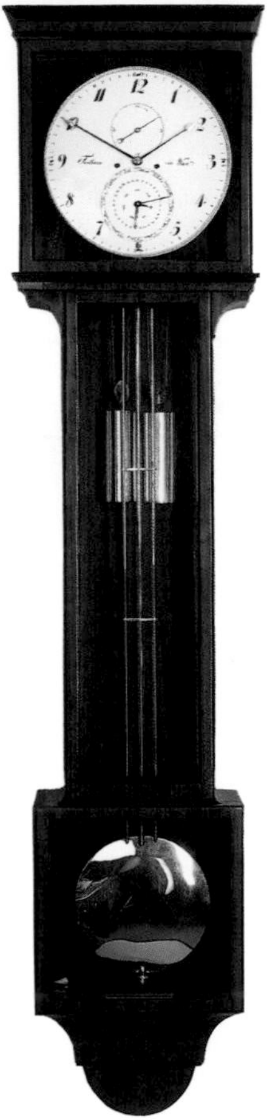

A Laterndluhr *with* grande sonnerie *striking by Joseph Fertbauer c.1820; ht 55in/140cm; value code A*

Identification checklist for *Laterndluhr* with complications

1. Is the dial round (and either enamelled or silvered and engraved brass)?
2. Are there two or more subsidiary dials?
3. Are there two steady screws at the bottom of the sides of the trunk?
4. Is the back unfinished? (i.e. not veneered)
5. Does the clock strike on two bells or gongs? (rather than a single bell or gong)
6. Are the front and sides glazed?
7. Is the piece signed on the dial?
8. Are the hands blued steel? (brass is used occasionally)

Clocks with "complications"
Among the finest Vienna regulators are the clocks with complications, so-called because these variations on the *Laterndluhr* have a number of subsidiary dials. These commonly show the day of the week, the date of the month or the month. The clock in the main picture shows all three on concentric rings within a large subsidiary dial (bottom), in addition to a seconds dial (top). Any clock with three subsidiary dials is highly desirable. They were made in small numbers c.1815-45, and are rare today. Some of the best makers are well-recorded; lesser makers are often unknown. Most clocks are in good condition.

The dial may be silvered and engraved brass or else enamelled, as on the example *above*, from a c.1820 *Laterndluhr* with *grande sonnerie* striking. This clock has a separate seconds dial and subsidiary dials for the day of the week and date. It was also produced by Fertbauer.
* Hands are generally made of blued steel, but brass is sometimes used. On the clock in the main picture, the steel hands have brass hearts on the tips.

Cases
The trunks are variations of the basic Viennese style. Tops may be flat or in the architectural style of *Laterndluhr* and *Dachluhr*. Mahogany is the most common veneer, but some cases are veneered with other woods or are ebonized. Decorative stringing in a pale-coloured wood is indicative of high quality.
* As well as the front, both sides are glazed. If a clock has a large bob, the sides at the bottom may be solid (not glazed) to avoid damage if the clock is moved.

Movements
Most are weight-driven, with a long pendulum and a dead beat anchor escapement (see p.173). They are of eight-day or one-month duration, and may strike on two bells or gongs.
* The seconds dial shows true seconds: cases were made longer than *Laterndluhr* cases, to make room for a seconds pendulum.

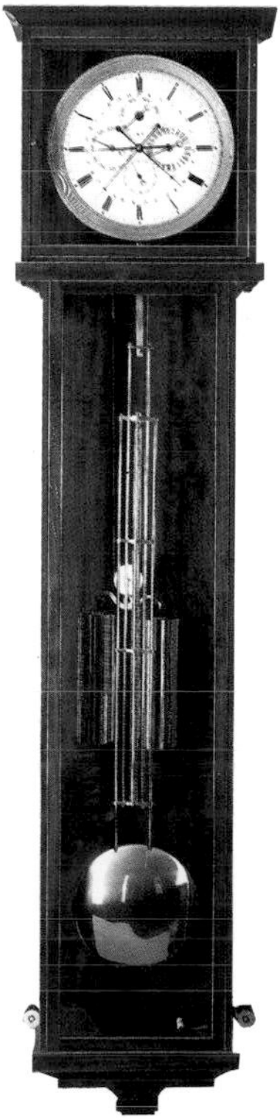

Unsigned clocks, like the c.1820 timepiece *above*, are uncommon: most clocks with complications are signed on the dial. The lack of a signature may detract slightly from value. This example, showing day, date and month, is of year duration – a rare feature.
* The steady screws at the bottom of the case are a typical Viennese feature (see p.155).
* The gridiron pendulum (see p.117), as on this example, is found on the best Vienna regulators. It serves to keep the pendulum length constant.

FLOOR REGULATORS

A floor-standing regulator of year duration by Johann Brandl c.1820; ht 75in/190.5cm; value code A

Identification checklist for Viennese floor-standing regulators
1. Is the case veneered with mahogany (or walnut)?
2. Is there an architectural top? (but some are flat-topped)
3. Are the front and sides of the case glazed?
4. Does the pendulum beat true seconds? (see below)
5. Is there a single weight?
6. Are there any subsidiary dials?
7. Are the hands blued steel? (and simple in shape)
8. Is the dial signed?

Floor-standing regulators
The development of the floor-standing, or longcase Viennese regulator took place during the same period as the production of wall regulators (see pp.154-9). However, floor-standing regulators were only a small part of the output of Viennese clockmakers.

Movements
The movements of floor-standing regulators are of superb quality. They are usually timepieces rather than striking clocks (and so have only one weight and one winding hole). Most are of eight-day duration, but some run for a month, three months or even a year before needing winding. Because of the height needed for the weight to fall, regulators of year-duration are always housed in a long case.

The dial
Floor-standing regulators always have a round dial. This may be enamelled or silvered brass, and either one-piece or with a separate chapter ring. The year-duration clock in the main picture has a subsidiary seconds dial. Two or three subsidiary dials, as on the clock at right, which shows day, date and seconds, are indicative of quality.

Hands are always blued steel and generally plain in appearance. There may be a counterpoise, either to the minute hand, or, as on the c.1825 walnut-veneered example with two-piece enamel dial shown *above*, both hands. On some hands, the tips may have small decorative motifs.

The pendulum
The pendulum consists of a steel rod with a large brass-faced bob. Unusually, floor-standing regulators beat true seconds, as the large case allowed a full-length seconds-beating pendulum to be fitted. By contrast, Vienna wall regulators usually beat only 45-50 seconds per minute.
* The beat scale, commonly fixed to the case interior on wall-hanging Vienna regulators (see p.157), is not always found on the floor-standing type.

The case
Mahogany is common, but there are a number of walnut cases. The architectural top, like that on the clock in the main picture, is typical. Most pieces have a simple plinth base.
* The front and sides are always glazed.
* As on the clock in the main picture, very fine decorative stringing – usually in light-coloured woods – is a feature indicative of high quality.

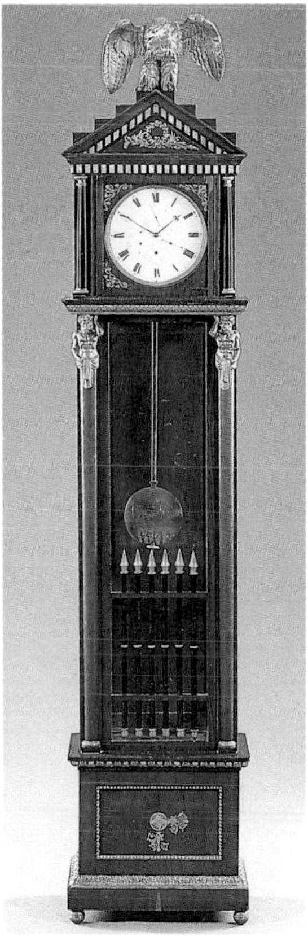

From the 1840s, cases tended to become more and more decorative, with increased use made of applied metal mouldings and mounts. The month-duration regulator shown *above*, produced by Joseph Brunner c.1840, is typical. The portcullis is a purely decorative touch.

NOVELTY CLOCKS

A Swiss automaton and musical chalet clock, c.1880

Novelty clocks have a history almost as long as that of clocks themselves: for centuries, clockmakers have tried to produce clocks that tell the time in unique ways, incorporate elaborate subsidiary indications or feature novel mechanical operations. Novelty clocks can be a fascinating area for the collector and the variety of styles and subject matter is enormous.

The earliest novelty clocks date back to the 17thC, when clocks themselves were a rarity. However, the vast majority that are available today were produced during the 19thC, mainly by French makers. There are a significant number of Swiss novelty clocks, and a number by English makers.

The mystery clock is one of the most famous and widely produced novelty clocks. Typically, this consists of a brass figure atop a marble base holding up a pendulum which swings apparently unconnected to the clock mechanism. There are many variations on the mystery theme, including figures holding a glass dial in which the hands move without any visible connection to the movement. In most mystery clocks, the spring-driven movement is inside the base.

Complex calendar and globe clocks are among the rarest novelty clocks. As well as the hours and minutes, they show astronomical and calendar information in unusual settings. Unlike most 19thC novelty clocks, globe clocks often have very complex movements. Because of their mechanical complexity, few were produced, and they can command high prices. If the mechanism is not functional, extensive (and costly) repairs may be involved.

During the 19thC, the great technological changes produced by the Industrial Revolution inspired a range of all-metal novelty clocks known as engineering and marine clocks. Modelled on heavy machinery, ships or other industrial themes, these clocks often incorporate working mechanical features, such as gears, hammers, pistons, or revolving lamps. The most famous style of marine clock shows a helmsman standing at the wheel of a ship. All examples were produced in France. Today, these are among the most collected of all novelty clocks.

Other popular types of novelty clock are those which make use of automaton figures (mechanical figures operated by a concealed mechanism). Automata work is closely associated with the quest for novelty, and automaton clocks – often with musical work – were extremely popular during the 19thC. The manufacture of automata was already highly developed in France, and so it seemed natural to fit working figures or other features in a clock mechanism. The clocks are often timepieces, or may strike the hours (and sometimes the half-hours) on a gong.

Although most automaton clocks were made by French (or Swiss) makers, there are a few English bracket and longcase clocks with automata and musical work, usually in the dial. Simple automata were also a popular feature of Black Forest wall clocks. (see p.105).

The makers of automaton clocks produced highly imaginative scenes, with a huge variety of subjects and mechanical features. Swiss makers produced novelty harbour scenes, the best of which include a rocking ship, turning windmill sails and water wheels, lapping waves and moving figures and horses. Very often, these scenes have musical accompaniment. These clocks have a simple, spring-driven clock movement. They were originally covered by a glass dome to protect the scenery, but this has often been lost.

Another unusual style of novelty clock, the picture clock, consists of a large oil painting – up to 36in/91cm in width – which shows a landscape with a village and a church tower. Set into the tower is an enamelled clock dial with a spring-driven movement. The simplest of these are timepieces, but more complicated examples strike the hours (and sometimes the quarter-hours) or operate a music box.

The variety of novelty clocks is almost endless. In many cases, the clock mechanism is not the most prominent or significant feature, as their appeal comes primarily from their unique indications or working features. All clocks should be in good mechanical condition: automaton figures are most vulnerable to damage. Any clock with automaton or musical work should be run before purchase, to make sure the mechanism is in good working order.

CURIOSITY AND MYSTERY CLOCKS

Curiosity and mystery clocks
Clockmakers have produced many kinds of curious clocks. In some cases, these simply look unusual; in others, they perform unusual functions as well as telling the time. The mystery clock (see right) also reflects the clockmaker's quest to develop new products for his customers. Almost all curiosity or mystery pieces date from the second half of the 19thC, and were made mainly in France.

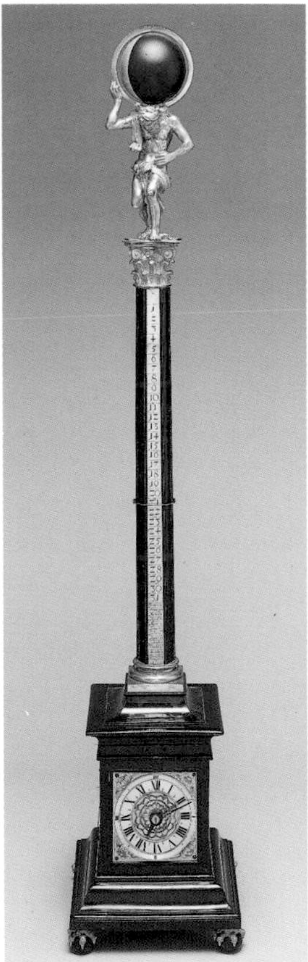

The German tortoiseshell and ormolu column clock, *above*, made in the late 17thC with verge escapement and striking movement, is extremely rare: few examples are known outside Germany. The figure of Hercules holding a revolving moon and the descending calendar ring are both controlled by the clock. The base of the column shows the maximum number of days in each month. Few 17thC novelty clocks survive.

Novelty clocks by English makers are uncommon. The only significant maker was Thomas Cole, who produced small travelling clocks, strut clocks (see pp.142-3) and other variations on traditional styles. Cole made many tripod clocks, like the c.1860 example *above*, in which the spirit level fixed to the plinth and the cupola with levelling plummet are used to ensure that the clock is level. Variations include a cooking pot suspended from three cast brass "logs"! All are timepieces. Tripod clocks are sought after by collectors, but they are not common.

The mystery clock
One of the most popular 19thC novelties is the mystery clock. The most common style shows a female figure holding a pendulum, which seems otherwise unconnected to the clock. However, the movement

causes the figure to rotate almost imperceptibly to the left and right. The motion set up causes the pendulum to swing, apparently unaided.

Like the c.1860 example shown *above*, the figure stands on a marble base containing the spring-driven movement. The figure may be bronze or spelter (a zinc alloy). A good bronze figure is indicative of a more valuable clock. Mystery clocks can be costly to overhaul.
* Some clocks have the maker's name, others only a stamped number or maker's mark.

The Art Deco jewelled "water clock" *above*, made for Cartier during the 1920s, is a modern variant on a 17thC mystery clock. The floating turtle moves around the chapter ring pointing to the hours, driven by a magnetic hour hand in the base.

Other mystery variations include a figure holding up a timepiece. On the rare bronze example *above*, produced c.1890 for Tiffany and Co., mystery features include the glass dial, the hands of which do not seem to be connected to the movement, which is in the urn held by the figure. Other variations include an elephant holding a timepiece in his trunk.

Collector's point
Because novelty clocks are so varied, with many examples produced as one-offs, there are few specific guidelines for the collector. Many novelty clocks are mechanical curiosities, so movements should be original and in good working order. Poorly executed repairs can reduce the value of a clock.

GLOBE CLOCKS

Globe and calendar clocks
Calendar indications are a common feature of many antique clocks, typically in the form of a date aperture or subsidiary calendar or moon dial. One distinctive form is the globe clock, often with complex calendar or astronomical indications. There are many variations on this type of novelty clock. For this reason, it is not possible to provide a checklist for them. Most were made in the 19thC, mainly by French or Swiss makers. Some were also made in Britain, Germany and the United States. Globe clocks are rare today.
* An 18thC forerunner of the globe clock was the orrery, a clockwork device showing the motion of the planets.

Movements
French 19thC globe clocks are generally spring-driven, and the movements are usually mass-produced. Most examples on the market are timepieces, and do not strike the hours.

On the French globe timepiece, *above*, produced c.1870, the terrestrial globe is mounted above a traditional spring-driven clock, which is itself fixed to a black marble base. The globe revolves once every 24 hours. Below the globe, a horizontally mounted disc indicating the month revolves once a year. The original *papier-mâché* globe is unlikely to have been lost, and any replacement would lower the value of the clock.
* Like French bracket clocks of the period (see p.82-3), dials are typically enamelled.

Signatures
The movements may be signed, although some simply bear a serial number. The dial is unlikely to have a signature, and late 19thC globe clocks may not be signed at all. On the example shown below left, the movement is signed (on an applied plaque) by J. Poncelet of Morez, in the Jura region. The Morbier-Morez district was a major centre of clockmaking in France.

Occasionally, the globe itself was used as the basis for the clock. Instead of astronomical or calendar indications, the mechanically complicated French globe clock, *above*, produced c.1740, has four clock dials and complex rack striking (see p.10). It also repeats the quarter-hours.
* The separate enamel cartouches bearing the numerals on the chapter ring are a typical feature of French clocks from the first half of the 18thC.

On the American perpetual calendar globe timepiece *above*, the terrestrial globe rotates once a day. The moulded base is engraved with a year calendar; the gilt chapter ring (with Roman numerals) of the clock revolves once yearly to show the date as well as the time. Few American globe timepieces are known. This example was patented in 1850 by Frederick S. Barnard of New York, the first American patent for a globe clock.

* Another American maker, the Swiss-born Louis Paul Juvet (1838-1930) of Glens Falls, New York, patented a clockwork "time globe" in 1867. Juvet's firm produced numerous globe clocks in which the revolutions of the Earth were correctly timed on the globe. Time elsewhere on Earth could be easily seen. The firm won many prizes for these clocks, which were produced in both table and floor-standing models. They were manufactured from 1878. However, Juvet's factory was destroyed by fire in 1886.

The globe clock shown *above* was made c.1800 by the London firm of Barrauds. It is essentially a skeleton clock, in the shape of a globe. The hour ring, at the "Equator", and the minute ring, at the "Tropic of Cancer" revolve at different rates. The time is shown against a fixed sun. The escapement is mounted horizontally inside the globe. The fusee is visible below the "Equator". English globe clocks of this kind are rare.

On the extremely rare German perpetual calendar and globe clock shown *left*, made in 1823 by J.C. Schuster of Ansbach, the terrestrial globe on the left shows the month, date and the times of sunrise and sunset. On the right, a celestial globe indicates the day of the month and the phases of the moon. The convex enamel dial shows 24 hours, with subsidiary dials provided for minutes and perpetual calendar.

Automaton clocks
Among the most fascinating novelty clocks are those with automata; that is, mechanical figures operated by hidden power. Their complexity suggests that they were intended for the exclusive end of the market.
* Because of their variety, it is not possible to provide a checklist for automaton clocks.
* Almost all 19thC automaton clocks are of eight-day duration, with spring-driven movements. Most do not strike the hours.

French and Swiss automaton clocks
Most 19thC automaton clocks were made c.1830-80, in France and Switzerland.

In keeping with the decorative nature of automaton clocks, the case (or frame) and the mechanism of the clock are generally elaborate or complicated. With its richly detailed village and harbour scene, the c.1880 Swiss enamel-dial novelty timepiece, *above*, is a typical example. When the musical movement plays a tune to mark the hour, a figure comes out of the church doors, the windmill sails turn and the ship rocks on the waves. Such timepiece movements are usually wound from the back; levers on the base are used to activate the the automaton mechanism.
* Complicated clocks like this one were also made in France. Domed clocks with ships on a stormy sea were popular.

Condition
If they have been well cared for, automaton clocks will still function as originally intended by their makers. Because the automaton work is often the most important feature of the clock, non-functional automata seriously affect the value of a clock. A common problem is surface damage. Although major damage to the mechanism is rare, there may be broken pins on the barrel which drives the automata.

The c.1850 ormolu clock with automaton musicians and tightrope walker, shown *above*, would have had a protective glass dome shaped to fit the wooden base, which contains the automaton mechanism. It is desirable to have the original dome, as it is difficult to obtain a replacement. The automata on this example are probably Swiss, but the clock is signed by Japy Frères, one of the largest 19thC French producers (see p.171).
* Although acrobats are common, it is unusual to find an automaton clock with a tightrope walker. Parading figures are more usual.

Other automaton clocks
Other 19thC variations include:
* carriage clocks with a singing bird inside a glass box
* automaton birds, monkeys or insects inside a glass dome
* musical boxes with figures (mainly Swiss).

A number of magician clocks were produced in France towards the end of the 19thC. Like the example shown *above*, these feature an automaton magician, who covers and then uncovers a "trick". This example is 33in/84cm in height. The two winding holes on the enamel dial indicate a striking clock. Because few were produced, magician clocks are sought after, despite the fact that neither the gilt-painted wood case nor the spring-driven clock movement are of high quality. On some examples, the magician figure stands on top of an ormolu or marble base.
* Magician clocks do not usually include musical work.

English automaton clocks
Automaton work is unusual, but not unknown, in late 18th and early 19thC English longcase and bracket clocks.

On this novelty wall clock *above*, exceptional for having automaton work, and produced c.1840 by James Lee of Bolton, Lancashire, the simple automaton waterwheel and windmill sails turn as the clock ticks. Together with its richly decorated dial surround, the clock is 20in/51cm in diameter. This example is very much a one-off, making it a particular collector's item. It comes from an area of England not otherwise known for clockmaking.
* Like other round-dial clocks (see pp.98-9), this example has a mahogany case, but the octagonal dial surround is inlaid with pewter. Brass was more often used for inlaid decoration, but mother-of-pearl and pewter were common c.1820-50, frequently combined with rosewood.
* For automaton work in English longcase clocks, see p.39.

If an English bracket clock has automata, then it may also have musical work. On the example *above*, made by John Marriott c.1775, horsemen move across the arch each hour, accompanied by the musical movement. Although this clock also strikes the quarter-hours – a repeat cord is visible on the right – the 20in/51cm case is no larger than most late 18thC brackets.
* Some arches may also contain an automata orchestra.
* Substantial numbers of automaton bracket clocks were produced for export to the Turkish and Chinese markets, during the late 18thC.

ENGINEERING AND MARINE CLOCKS

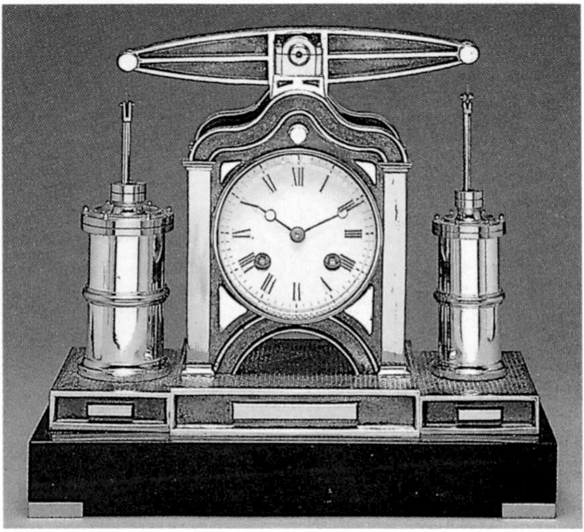

A French beam engine clock, with movement stamped "G.L.T." c.1880; ht 9½in/24cm; value code E

Because of the huge variety of subjects and mechanical features, it is not possible to provide an identification checklist for engineering and marine clocks. Identification and assessment is largely a matter of experience – collectors should try to handle as many types as possible.

Engineering and marine clocks
Clocks featuring machinery or marine subjects are among the most popular novelty clocks. Probably inspired by the Industrial Revolution, these clocks were produced mainly during the second half of the 19thC (and the early 20thC). They were made almost exclusively in France. Engineering and marine clocks were exported to Britain in fairly large quantities, but never achieved the popularity enjoyed there by carriage clocks. Because these clocks were produced relatively recently, both frame and movements are generally still in good condition. No fakes are known.

Subjects
Typical subjects include industrial themes, such as steam-driven machinery, lighthouses or the bridge of a ship. Each example has a mechanical operation to complement the type of machine featured. In the beam engine clock in the main picture, the beam forms the pendulum and each of the flanking cylinders contains a bob. Although mass-produced, engineering and marine clocks are generally well made.
* Size varies considerably, with some examples as much as 20in/50cm tall.

The frame
The frame is typically brass or bronze (sometimes both) and often has silvered or silver-plated segments to provide a contrast between the metal parts. The clocks are generally mounted on a black marble base or plinth. Small brass pad feet are a common feature. Backs are usually well finished.

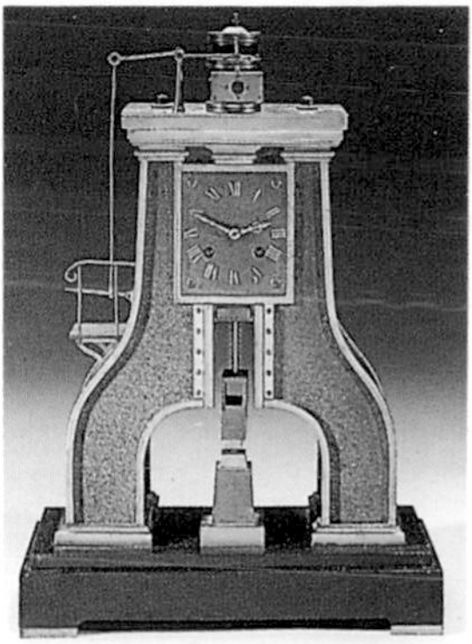

On the gilt and bronze hammer clock shown *above* – one of the most popular styles of engineering clocks – the bronze is patinated to give the effect of iron, in keeping with the industrial theme. This type of clock has a U-shaped pendulum, which swings inside the hollow legs. The hammer rises and falls with the action of the pendulum.
* Engineering and marine clocks are frequently not signed on the dial, but may be signed on the movement, which may also be numbered. The movement of the clock above is signed "Japy Frères". This Paris firm was a significant maker of carriage clocks and various types of machinery. On the clock in the main picture, the movement was also made by Japy Frères, but is stamped "G.L.T., Paris".

Perhaps the most popular motif used on engineering or marine clocks was the helmsman on the stern of a ship. As on the 12in/30cm-high example *above*, the movement is connected to the figure of the helmsman, who sways from side to side with the beating of the seconds.

Movements

Many engineering and marine clocks are timepieces only. Examples which strike the hours most commonly do so on a bell. All examples are of eight-day duration, either with a short pendulum or a platform lever escapement (see p.10). The mass-produced movements are usually in good working order.

The dial

The dial varies considerably, and may be enamel, like the example in the main picture, or brass (either one-piece or with an applied chapter ring). On the hammer clock shown left, the dial is patinated to match the rest of the frame. Numerals are usually Roman.

As well as additional features such as an aneroid barometer, thermometer and compass, the revolving ship's lantern timepiece *above*, produced c.1890, has two silvered clock dials, with applied chapter rings. A separate movement mounted in the bollard drives the lantern.

GLOSSARY

Act of Parliament clock Popular alternative name for the 18thC wall-hanging tavern clock; so-called because an Act passed by the English Parliament in 1797 placed a tax on all privately-owned clocks, reputedly bringing about a great need for public timepieces.
Alarm A part of a clock mechanism which can be set so that the clock strikes at a predetermined time.
Anchor escapement A type of escape mechanism, shaped like an anchor, which engages at precise intervals with the toothed escape wheel. The anchor permits the use of a pendulum (either long or short), and gives greater accuracy than was possible with the verge escapement. Supposedly invented c.1670 by Robert Hooke or William Clement.
Arabesque A form of scrolling marquetry inlay, found typically on longcases from c.1700-10 (and, more rarely, on bracket clock cases).
Arbor The round steel spindle or shaft on which a wheel, pinion, lever or anchor is mounted.
Arch Incorporated into clock dials – initially on longcases – from c.1715.
Architectural top A decorative hood top in the form of a Classical pediment.
Automaton clock A clock with figures that move or strike at predetermined times.
Backcock A metal apron (often engraved or pierced) covering the top of the pendulum rod on some English bracket clocks.
Backplate Together with the frontplate, one of the two vertically aligned plates between which the clock movement is supported.
Balance A type of escape mechanism, consisting of an oscillating wheel, mounted above the clock movement, which controls the going of the clock. Used on clocks that do not have a pendulum.
Balloon clock A type of bracket clock, with a shape similar to a hot-air balloon; often veneered with satinwood.
Banjo clock A type of American wall clock, shaped like the musical instrument it is named for, made by the Willard family during the early 19thC. The term "banjo" also refers to some tavern clocks, usually with lacquered cases.
Barrel The cylindrical brass box containing the mainspring (on spring-driven clocks). On weight-driven clocks, the line on which the weight is hung is wound around the barrel.
Base The bottom section of a longcase clock.
Basket top An ornamental top made of gilt metal or silver and usually elaborately pierced. The basket top was used mainly on early English bracket clocks.
Beat A clock is "in beat" when the escape wheel produces a regular and even "tick-tock". If it is not in beat, the clock will require adjustment.
Beat scale A graduated scale, fixed to the case interior of many Vienna regulators, and used to measure the regularity of the pendulum swing.
Bell The metal dome on which clocks and alarms strike. On most antique clocks, the bell is made of a copper-tin alloy known as "bell metal".
Bell top The smoothly curved top of a bracket clock, commonly found on mahogany cases from the second half of the 18thC.
Bezel The ring which surrounds the dial, and secures the glass dial cover. The bezel is usually made of brass, but there are some wooden examples.
"Bird and flower" A form of marquetry inlay, usually in oval reserves, showing a bird surrounded by foliage.
Bob The disc-shaped weight at the bottom of the pendulum rod. The bob is usually made of lead, with an outer casing of brass. In bracket, English dial and lantern clocks – all with a verge escapement – the bob is frequently pear-shaped.
Bolt and shutter Found in early longcase clocks, and used to keep the clock going during winding. Shutters close the winding holes while the clock is running. To open these shutters to enable winding to take place, a lever or a cord is pulled which activates the maintaining power.
***Bombé* case** A case which swells outward, either at the trunk or the base section. *Bombé* cases are most common on French and Dutch longcases.

Boulle case A form of marquetry, combining metal (usually brass) with tortoiseshell. It takes its name from the great French casemaker, Charles-André Boulle.
Bracket clock A type of spring-driven clock, sometimes known as a mantel or shelf clock, designed to stand on a surface.
Break arch (or broken arch) Another name for the arch at the top of the dial on bracket or longcase clocks.
Bun feet A type of foot used on early longcases; fixed to the bottom of the case by means of pegs. Shallow bun feet are also found on 19thC four-glass or mantel clocks.
Caddy top Used on many early longcase clocks; the caddy top is shaped like a tea container.
Calendar aperture A rectangular (sometimes round or semi-circular) opening in the surface of the dial, through which the date is shown.
Capital The top or bottom of a column (or quarter-column), usually made of brass (some are gold-leafed wood) on the hood or trunk of a longcase clock.
Carriage clock A small, spring-driven clock, produced mainly by French makers during the 19thC. The basic frame is always brass.
Cartel clock A type of spring-driven wall-hung clock, produced mainly in France during the 18thC.
Cartouche On longcase clocks, the engraved scroll with rolled-up ends, in which the maker's name is inscribed.
Case The protective and often ornamental covering which encloses a clock.
Centre seconds hand A seconds hand pivoted at the centre of the dial. An alternative to a separate subsidiary dial for seconds.
Chamfer top A sloping top, sometimes with bevelled edges, found on certain English bracket clocks of the early 19thC. Often surmounted by a cast brass finial in the form of a pineapple.
Chapter ring The circular ring on the dial, on which the hours and minutes are engraved, attached or painted.
Chinoiserie Oriental-style decorative motifs; found on lacquered and painted cases.
Chronometer A common name for marine chronometers – extremely precise timekeepers designed for use at sea.
Clock garniture A set of ornaments for the mantelpiece, comprising a clock and flanking candelabra. Produced mainly in France.
Collet A dome-shaped ring, or washer, used to secure the clock hands, and held in place by a tapered steel pin; also refers to the stepped collar used to attach a wheel to an arbor.
***Comtoise* clock** Longcase clocks produced by provincial French makers, mainly during the 19thC. Cases are usually pine, with a bulbous trunk.
Count wheel Also known as a locking plate; a wheel with segments cut out of the edge or with pins fitted to one face, which controls the striking of a clock.
Crazing A network of fine cracks found on enamel or painted metal dials.
Cresting Applied ornament, such as pierced wood or *repoussé* metal, fixed to the hood or top.
Crossbanding Veneers laid at right angles to the main case veneer, possibly along edges.
Crossings A term used by clockmakers for the spokes of wheels. Five or more crossings is a good sign of quality.
Crown wheel The horizontally mounted escape wheel used in a verge escapement.
Crutch A rod attached at the top to the pallet arbor, and with a fork, slot or pin which engages with the pendulum.
Cuckoo clock Decorative carved wooden wall clocks produced in the Black Forest. They feature a mechanical cuckoo which calls when the clock strikes the hours.
Cushion top A rounded top found on many early English bracket clocks.
Cut-out A section of the dial cut away to reveal the surface underneath; a cut-out may also contain automaton figures.
Cylinder escapement A form of platform escapement, invented in 1695 by Thomas Tompion; fitted to many carriage clocks in the 19thC.
Dead beat escapement A type of **anchor escapement**, invented by George Graham, and similar to the **recoil escapement**. The pallets are shaped in such a way that there is no recoil when they engage the teeth of the escape wheel. Used in precise clocks such as regulators.

Dial The "face" of a clock, which shows the time. Dials may be metal, wood or enamel.
Dial clock A type of English wall clock with a round dial, of engraved brass, painted wood or painted iron. All are spring-driven, and usually have a **fusee movement**. Most are timepieces and do not strike the hours. The main variation is the trunk-dial clock.
Dial feet The pillars which attach the dial to the frontplate of the movement (or, on some longcases, to the **falseplate).**
Dial mask A rectangular brass plate – cut out in the centre – sometimes with engine-turned decoration, fitted around the dial on many carriage clocks.
Dialplate The metal plate to which the chapter ring and spandrels are attached.
Duration The period for which a clock runs between winding.
Enamel A coloured glassy substance, usually opaque, fused to the surface of a metal dial.
Endless rope (or chain) A type of winding mechanism, used typically on clocks of 30-hour duration. It consists of a loop of rope or chain running through a series of pulleys connected to the train, with a single weight to provide power.
Engine-turning Decorative patterns, usually around or on the dial, created by being turned and inscribed on a machine.
Escapement That part of the clock that regulates it, and transmits the impulse of the wheel train to the pendulum or balance.
Escape wheel The wheel which engages with the pallets.
Escutcheon A brass plate surrounding and protecting the edges of a keyhole – sometimes with a cap or cover on a pivot.
Falseplate A metal plate, with pillars, used on painted-dial longcases to secure the dial to the frontplate.
False pendulum See mock pendulum aperture.
Feet The shaped or moulded features fixed to the base of the clock.
Finial Brass or wooden ornament, frequently of "ball and spire" pattern, applied to the top of a clock.
Fish-scale fret Pierced brass or gilded metal panels shaped like the scales of a fish and set into the sides of the case.
Foliot A bar with small adjustable weights attached, which acts as a balance in a **verge escapement** . The foliot appears only on the very earliest domestic clocks.
Four-glass A small bracket clock, with glass on all four sides of the case.
Fret A pierced section of the hood of a longcase clock or the case of a bracket clock. Frets are usually backed with silk, which allows the sound of the bell to escape. Frets may be wood (which is fragile) or brass, sometimes in the form of "fish-scales".
Fusee A conical spool that evens out the uneven pull of a mainspring as it unwinds. The fusee is used to ensure accurate timkeeping. It was commonly used on English bracket clocks, dial clocks, English carriage clocks and marine chronometers.
Gesso A plaster-like substance applied to cases before gilding or painting. Sometimes known as "raised work", where it is built up to form part of the decoration.
Gimbals The pivoted rings used in marine chronometer boxes to keep the chronometer level.
Going barrel A cylindrical brass drum containing the mainspring. The going barrel is toothed on its periphery, so that it can transmit power directly to the wheels of the train. The going barrel is used in clocks which do not have a fusee movement.
Going train The set of wheels which drives the clock.
Gong Used instead of a bell for the striking mechanism of many 19thC clocks, especially carriage clocks. Usually the gong is a coiled steel wire.
Grande sonnerie A type of striking mechanism, which strikes the hours and quarter-hours, and then repeats the previous hour struck at each quarter.
Great wheel The first and largest wheel in a clock train.
Gridiron pendulum A type of pendulum rod used on very accurate clocks such as regulators. The gridiron consists of up to nine rods of alternating brass and steel. The rods expand or contract in different directions with changes in temperature, ensuring that the length of the pendulum remains the same, and that the timekeeping of the

clock is not affected.
Gut Used on some bracket clocks for the line connecting the barrel to the fusee.
Hammer Fitted to clocks which strike the hours; this consists of an arm with a weight on the end, which strikes the bell or gong at intervals dictated by the striking mechanism.
Hands Pointers which indicate the exact hour and minute; made of brass or blued steel, and often elaborately pierced or shaped. They are fixed to a pipe projecting through the dial centre.
Hood The top part of a longcase clock. The hood is detachable to provide access to the movement. Early longcases had a rising hood. from the end of the 17thC, hoods were made to slide forward, and fitted with a glazed hinged door.
Inverted bell top The opposite of the bell top; features an outward-swelling, instead of a concave centre; used on bracket clocks from c.1715.
"Ivory" A small circular panel, originally made of ivory, set into the case of a marine chronometer, and bearing the maker's name and the serial number of the clock.
Journeyman A clockmaker who has finished his apprenticeship.
Lacquerwork Also known as "japanning". Layers of varnish used as a ground for Chinoiserie decoration. Used on some English longcase and bracket clocks.
Lantern clock The earliest English domestic clock; with all-brass case and dial. All are weight-driven, with striking mechanism and, sometimes, an alarm.
Leaves The "teeth" of a **pinion.**
Lenticle Also known as "bull's eye". The round glass section in the trunk door of a longcase clock, through which the motion of the pendulum bob can be seen.
Lever escapement A type of escape mechanism which uses a pivoted lever to connect the pallets and the balance wheel. The lever escapement was generally used on travelling clocks, chronometers and the best four-glass bracket clocks.
Lines Wires of gut, rope or steel, on which the pulleys and weights are hung.
Locking Plate See count wheel.
Longcase clock A weight-driven, floor-standing clock with an anchor escapement and a long, seconds pendulum. Typically of eight-day duration.
Loud/soft lever A lever mounted on the side of the case, which allows the strike to be switched from loud to soft; found on some late 18thC and early 19thC English bracket clocks.
Mainspring The coiled steel spring that, when wound, provides the power for the wheels of the going and striking trains in a spring-driven clock.
Maintaining Power A simple device to ensure that power continues to be applied to the **going train**, by means of a spring-loaded lever, while the clock is being wound. This means that the clock does not stop and thus need to be re-set to time after winding. Maintaining power is most often found in very precise clocks such as regulators and chronometers.
Mantel clock A small bracket or table clock, typically in a rosewood, mahogany or ebonized wood case; produced mainly in the first half of the 19thC.
Marine chronometer Extremely accurate spring-driven timepieces, developed for use at sea to enable accurate determination of longitude. Chronometers may be of one-, two- or eight-day duration.
Marquetry Decorative inlay using woods of various grain, colour and figuring. Used on early longcase clocks and very occasionally on bracket clocks .
Masking frame The wooden frame overlapping the edges of the **dialplate.**
Matting A distinctive hammered finish found on the dial centre of many English longcase and bracket clocks.
Mercury jar A type of pendulum bob used on very accurate clocks, and intended to compensate for changes in temperature, which can affect timekeeping. The mercury in the jar rises as temperature increases, raising the centre of oscillation of the pendulum as the length of the rod increases.
Mock pendulum aperture An opening in the dial of some bracket clocks, which shows the motion of the pendulum by means of a rod connected to the escapement.

Moon dial A subsidiary dial, usually fitted in the arch of a longcase clock (or, very rarely, a bracket clock), to show the phases of the moon.
Motion work The wheels and pinions that carry the drive from the movement to the hands.
Movement All the parts of a clock mechanism which lie behind the dial. The movement is usually made of brass, with some steel parts. However, early American clocks were often made with wooden plates and wheels. Wood was also used in Germany, Austria and Switzerland.
Mystery clock Principally 19thC novelty clocks, usually with a figure holding a pendulum which seems to swing unaided.
Ogee An S-shaped case moulding.
Ormolu Gilded or gold-coloured metal
"Oyster" veneer Distinctive rounded sections of veneer, formed by cutting across the full width of the olive tree.
Pad feet Shallow oblong or round feet fixed to the bottom of the case.
Pagoda top A decorative top, used mainly on longcase clocks, reflecting Oriental architecture.
Pallets An arm in the escape mechanism that checks the motion of the escape wheel by intermittently engaging with the teeth of the wheel.
Parquetry Geometrical marquetry inlay formed from small pieces of veneer; found on some 17thC longcases.
Passing strike A striking mechanism operated directly from the **going train**. It causes a hammer to strike a bell once every hour.
Pedestal clock A large bracket clock mounted on a matching pedestal, usually stood on the floor or against a wall. Produced in France from the late 17th to the mid-18thC.
Pendule d'officier (officer's clock). A small, portable spring-driven timepiece, produced in France during the 18thC.
Pendule religieuse (''church'' clock) Bracket clocks produced in France during the late 17thC. The name comes from their resemblance to religious architecture.
Pendulum A swinging metal or wood rod with a flat or bulbous bob fixed to the end; the movement controls the action of the escape mechanism. The pendulum swings at a fixed rate and controls the timekeeping of the clock.
Petite sonnerie A type of striking mechanism in which the clock strikes the hours and quarter-hours, but usually repeats ***grande sonnerie***.
Pillar The brass rods which hold the two plates of the movement together.
Pin wheel escapement A type of escape mechanism in which the pallets of a narrow anchor arm engage semi-circular pins on the side of the escape wheel (rather than the usual teeth). Commonly used on 18thC French clocks.
Pinion A small, toothed steel wheel which engages with a larger wheel.
Pivot The ends of an arbor, which are supported in pivot holes in the plates.
Platform Common in carriage clocks; consists of a horizontally mounted plate with the lever escapement mounted on it.
Plinth The base of a longcase clock.
Quarter strike Also known as quarter chiming. A form of striking mechanism, in which each quarter-hour is struck on a number of bells or gongs.
Rack striking A system of striking in which the striking mechanism is regulated by the position of the hands. This allows the strike to be repeated without it getting out of sequence.
Rating nut An adjustable nut below the pendulum bob, on a threaded section of the rod. The rating nut is used to raise or lower the bob, in order to correct the timekeeping of the clock.
Recoil escapement A type of anchor escapement, in which the escape wheel recoils slightly as each tooth escapes from the pallets.
Regulation dial A subsidiary dial which permits adjustments to be made to the length of the pendulum.
Regulator An extremely accurate clock, used as a standard by which other clocks may be set. Regulators may be longcase or wall-hanging, and either weight- or spring-driven.
Repeating work A device which enables the last hour (or the hour and quarter-hour) to be struck again when a cord is pulled or a

button is pressed.
Rise and fall A regulating mechanism, by which the length of the pendulum rod can be altered by moving a pointer or hand on the dial.
Roman striking A form of striking in which the hours are struck with a reduced number of blows.
Salt box The wooden box behind the dial of some early English wall clocks, which contains the movement.
Seatboard The wooden board on which the movement of a longcase or bracket clock is mounted.
Shelf clock The American term for bracket or mantel clocks.
Silvered brass Brass that is coloured silver by the application of a silvering compound.
Skeleton clock A clock with the plates pierced and cut away in order to display as much of the working parts as possible.
Spandrels A decorative feature – applied cast brass, engraved or painted – found in the corners of the dial or the arch.
Spotting A distinctive hatched pattern found on the plates of some marine chronometers.
Spring detent escapement A variation or improvement on the **lever escapement** which was used on marine chronometers and the best English carriage clocks; commonly known as the "chronometer escapement".
Steady screw One of two adjustable screws mounted on plates on the sides of the cases of Vienna wall regulators; used to hold the clock level.
Strike/silent A lever or hand on the dial which enables the striking mechanism to be shut off without affecting the running of the clock.
Striking train The system of wheels and pinions which, when set in motion cause the clock to strike.
Stringing Fine inlaid lines – usually in brass or light-coloured wood – found on decorative cases.
Subsidiary dial A small dial contained within the main clock dial, typically showing seconds, date or strike/silent indication.
Suspension spring The device by which the pendulum is hung; consists of a short steel spring attached to a block at the top of the backplate.
Tallcase clock The term used in the United States for a longcase clock.
Tavern clock A weight-driven wall clock, with a large dial and a long trunk. The case is usually lacquered, and decorated with Chinoiserie on a black ground. There are some mahogany-veneered cases.
Thirty-hour clock A clock which must be wound daily, with a margin of six hours in case of delay in rewinding.
Timepiece Any clock which tells the time only, with no striking mechanism.
Train An interconnected series of wheels and pinions, which transmits power from a mainspring or weights to the escape mechanism and the hands.
Trunk The middle section of a long case; the trunk may be solid or glazed, and usually has a door at the front.
Trunk-dial A spring-driven wall clock with a round dial and a trunk containing a pendulum below the dial. Sometimes known as a "drop dial".
Twist columns A decorative feature found on many 17thC English longcase clocks, and occasionally on bracket clocks.
Up/down dial A subsidiary dial, commonly found on marine chronometers, which indicates how much time remains before the clock must be wound.
Veneer A thin layer of wood applied over the carcass of a clock.
Verge A rod with two flag-shaped pallets, which engages the crown wheel in a verge escapement.
Verge escapement Also known as a "crown wheel escapement". The oldest form of escape mechanism. Typical feature is the short pendulum with bulbous bob.
Verre eglomisé (reverse-painted glass) A decorative feature commonly used by makers in the United States; features animals, plants, geometric patterns or patriotic or historical motifs.
Vienna regulator Extremely precise and finely made weight-driven clocks – either wall-hanging or floor-standing – produced in Austria during the first half of the 19thC.
Wagon-spring A wide spring made up of steel leaves. Provides the motive power in some American shelf clocks.

SELECTED MAKERS AND MANUFACTURERS

Dates refer to known working dates, unless marked "b." (for birth) or "d." (for death). Place names refer to where a maker was most active. Most makers signed or marked their clocks (sometimes in Latin).

Allam and Clements (1764-95)
London. Produced mainly longcase and bracket clocks.

Ansonia Clock Co. (1851-c.1930)
Ansonia, Connecticut. This firm mass-produced weight-driven shelf and wall clocks in the second half of the 19thC.

Arnold, John (1783-99)
London. One of the most famous English makers of marine chronometers. Produced models of one-, two-, and eight-day duration.

Auguste, (active from 1840)
Paris. Produced carriage clocks.

Bagnall, Benjamin (b.1689-d.1773)
Boston, Massachusetts. The first clockmaker in Boston; produced tallcase clocks.

Banger, Edward (1695-1713)
London. Nephew of, and assistant to Thomas Tompion.

Barraud family (1796-1825)
London. This firm is best-known for marine chronometers.

Barwise, John (1790-1842)
London. Produced clocks and watches.

Birge and Fuller (1844-48)
Bristol, Connecticut. Partnership of John Birge and Thomas Fuller; produced many "Steeple" shelf clocks.

Boulle, Charles-Andre (b.1642 -d.1732)
Paris. Gave his name to a particular form of marquetry.

Bowyer, William (1626-47)
London. A maker of fine lantern clocks.

Bradley, Langley (1695-1738)
London. Famous maker of lantern and longcase clocks, and also watches.

Breguet, Abraham-Louis (1747-1823)
Paris. Probably the finest of all French clockmakers. Designed the first carriage clocks; also produced marine chronometers and watches. In business until the 1950s.

Brewster and Ingrahams (1842-52)
Bristol, Connecticut. Prolific producers of shelf clocks.

Brocot, Achille and Louis-Gabriel (active 19thC)
Paris. Produced carriage clocks, some with enamel panels; introduced new escapements.

Burnap, Daniel (b.1759-d.1838)
East Windsor and Coventry, Connecticut. Important early American maker of tallcase clocks, some with musical work.

Chandlee family (active late 17thC-early 19thC)
Philadelphia, Pennsylvania and Baltimore, Maryland. Included Benjamin, Goldsmith and Isaac. Produced mainly tallcase clocks.

Charmes, Simon de (1671-1730)
London. A Huguenot (French Protestant) refugee, noted for bracket and longcase clocks.

Clay family (1730-50)
London. Clock and watch makers.

Clement (also Clements), William (1677-99)
London. One of the first English makers to use the anchor escapement, c.1676; developed the recoil escapement (see p.176). Became Master of the Clockmakers' Company in 1694.

Clowes, James (1671-89)
London. Well-known maker of longcase clocks; also produced some bracket clocks, including fine ebony-veneered examples.

Cole, Thomas (b.1800-64)
London. Produced ornamental spring-driven timepieces of the highest quality, including carriage, strut, and novelty clocks.

Condliff family (1816-67)
Liverpool. Produced all types of clocks, but renowned as the finest makers of English skeleton clocks. Included founder, James, also Joseph, John and Thomas. Firm lasted until 1923.

Cottey, Abel (1655-1711)
Philadelphia, Pennsylvania. The first authenticated clockmaker in America. Made tallcase clocks with movements of eight-day duration.

Cowan, James (1744-81)
Edinburgh. One of the best known Scottish longcase makers.

Coxeter, Nicholas (1646-79)
London. One of the finest makers of early lantern clocks.

Crane, Aaron (1840-70)
Caldwell, New Jersey. Patented a clock of one-year duration.

Cumming Alexander (1781-1814)
Edinburgh and London. Noted for the production of watches, bracket clocks and marine chronometers.

Curtis, Lemuel (1790-1857)
Concord, Massachusetts. One of the finest American makers. Produced banjo, *Girandole*, lyre and shelf clocks.

Delander, Daniel(1699-1733)
London. A fine maker of clocks and watches.

Dejardin (19thC)
Paris, Produced fine panelled carriage clocks.

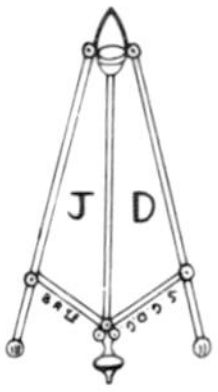

Dent, Edward John (1790-1853)
London. famous maker of all types of clock.

Drocourt, Pierre and Alfred (1860-89)
Paris. Makers of some of the finest carriage clocks, including panelled examples.

Dutton, William (1746-94)
London. Partner with and successor to Thomas Mudge; produced some of the finest longcase clocks.

Dutton, Matthew and Thomas (1799-1804)
London. Sons of William Dutton and noted makers of longcase, bracket and wall clocks.

Dwerrihouse, John (1773-1805)
London. Produced bracket, wall and tavern clocks, and some longcases.

Dwerrihouse and Carter (1802-23)
London. Continued the tradition of John Dwerrihouse.

Earnshaw, Thomas (1749-1829)
London. One of the most important makers of marine chronometers.

East, Edward (1610-93)
London. The most celebrated of early English makers. Produced watches, longcase clocks, bracket clocks and lantern clocks.

Ebsworth, John (1665-1703)
London. Good maker of lantern, bracket and longcase clocks, and also watches.

Eiffe, James (b.1800-d.1880)
London. A fine chronometer maker.

Ellicott, John (1696-1733)
London. A noted watchmaker.

Ellicott, John (b.1706-d.1772)
London. Son of the above maker, and one of the most important English makers of watches and clocks. Inventor of a compensated pendulum which avoided the need to raise or lower the bob.

Ellicott and Taylor (1811-30)
London. Succeeded John Ellicott. Produced bracket clocks and watches.

Elsner and Petrovits (c.1820-40)
Vienna. Produced Vienna regulators, particularly *Dachluhr*.

Emmery, Josiah (1781-97)
London. A very good maker of bracket clocks and watches.

Evans W.F and Sons (1850-1900)
Handsworth. Prolific makers of skeleton clocks; many signed by a retailer.

Finney, Joseph (c.1708-72)
Liverpool. Produced high quality longcases, regulators and astronomical clocks.

French, Santiago (1810-1840)
London. Produced clocks and watches extensively for the Spanish market.
Frodsham family
London-based firm, included Charles and William James.
Frodsham, Charles (1810-40)
London. Noted maker of marine chronometers of two- and eight-day duration, and watches.
Frodsham, William James (1802-1850)
London. Produced watches and clocks.
Fromanteel, Ahasuerus (1663-85)
London. A famous maker of longcases; supposedly the first to make pendulum clocks in England.
Fromanteel, John (1663-81)
London. Son of Ahasuerus; assisted in the establishment of the pendulum clock.

Ganthony, Richard (1794-1845)
London. Produced longcases, brackets and wall clocks; also watches.
Garnier, Paul (b.1801-d.1869)
Paris. Important early producer of carriage clocks. Succeeded by son Paul (active late 19thC).
Gould, Christopher (1682-1718)
London. A very important maker of longcase clocks.

Graham, George (1695-1751)
London. One of the most renowned English makers. Produced longcases and some lantern clocks. Became assistant to Thomas Tompion; buried with him in Westminster Abbey.

Grant, John (1781-1810)
London. A good maker of bracket clocks and watches, but produced few longcases.
Grant, John (1817-67)
London. Son of the above maker. Produced numerous wall clocks.

Gray, Benjamin (b.1676-d.1764)
London. Clockmaker to George II; formed partnership with his son-in-law Justin Vulliamy as Gray and Vulliamy (1743-62). Produced watches and bracket clocks.
Gray, James (1765-1806)
Edinburgh. A good maker of longcase clocks.
Gretton, Charles (1672-1733)
London. A fine maker of longcase, lantern and bracket clocks; also watches.
Grignion, Daniel and Thomas (1730-50)
London. Good makers of bracket clocks and watches; previously employed by Daniel Quare.
Haley, Charles (1781-1825)
London. A well-known maker of chronometers, bracket clocks and watches.
Haley and Milner (1799-1815)
London. Partnership which produced bracket clocks, wall clocks and watches.
Hamilton Watch Co. (1892-1955)
Lancaster, Pennsylvania. Produced large numbers of marine chronometers for the U.S. Navy.
Handley and Moore (1802-24)
London. Firm produced bracket clocks and round dial wall clocks.
Harland, Thomas (b.1735-d.1807)
Norwich, Connecticut. Produced a variety of clocks; apprentices included Daniel Burnap.
Harrison, John (b.1693-d.1766)
Barrow and London. Developed the first marine chronometer, also invented the "gridiron" compensated pendulum.
Herbert, Cornelius (1667-89)
London. A good maker of bracket clocks and watches.
Higgs and Evans (1775-1825)
London. Firm which made bracket clocks, often with three trains or musical work; many for the Spanish market.
Hodges, Nathaniel (1681-95)
London. Produced mainly bracket clocks.
Holmes, John (1762-1815)
London. One of the most important English makers of longcase clocks. Favoured a wood pendulum rod for accurate timekeeping.
Hubert, David (1714-48)
London. A good maker of both clocks and watches.
Howden, James (1764-1810)
Edinburgh. A good maker of longcase clocks.

Ives, Joseph (1810-55)
Bristol, Connecticut. A pioneer of the American clock industry. Invented the "wagon spring" shelf clock.
Jacot, Henri (1855-1900)
Paris. One of the finest and most prolific makers of carriage clocks.

Japy Frères (1772-early 20thC)
Badevel, Beaucourt and Paris. Included Frédéric (1749-1813), Adolphe (1813-97) and Maurice (active from c.1860). One of the largest French makers, particularly of decorative carriage clocks. Pioneered the mass production of clocks.

Jerome, Chauncey (1816-55)
New Haven and Bristol, Connecticut. Important American maker; Produced cases for Eli Terry, including earliest "pillar and scroll" shelf clock; mass-produced 30-hour and eight-day shelf clocks.
Jessner, Joseph (c.1820-30)
Vienna. Produced very fine *Laterndluhr* (lantern-case regulators).
Jones, Henry (1663-d.1695)
London. One of the finest early makers of longcase and bracket clocks; also watches.

Jules (dates unknown)
Paris. An early maker of carriage clocks.
Kaufmann, Kaspar (c.1815-c.1850)
Vienna. Produced fine *Dachluhr* (rooftop-case regulators), as well as seconds-beating regulators with *grande sonnerie.*
Kipling, William (1705-37)
London. A fine maker of longcase and bracket clocks, also watches.
Knibb, John (b.1650-d.1722)
Oxford. One of four Knibb brothers. Younger brother of Joseph, for whom he made many clocks. Also produced longcase, bracket, wall and lantern clocks under his own name.

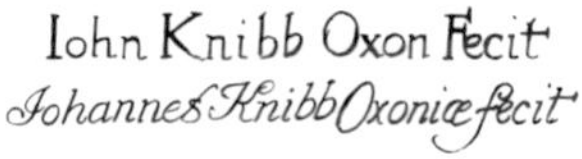

Knibb, Joseph (b.1670-d.1711)
London and Oxford. One of the finest and most prolific English makers of longcase, bracket, wall-hanging and lantern clocks. Invented the "Roman" striking mechanism.

Knibb, Peter (b.1651-c.1679)
London. Apprenticed to Joseph Knibb, his cousin. Only two clocks by Peter are known.
Knibb, Samuel (b.1663-d.1670)
Another cousin of Joseph Knibb; only three clocks by him are known.
Knottesford, William (1663-96)
London. A good maker of bracket and longcase clocks.
Kullberg, Victor (1850-90)
London. This Swedish-born maker produced some of the finest English marine chronometers and watches.
Le Roy (c.1785-20thC)
Paris. An important French maker of clocks and watches.
Litherland, Davies and Co. (1818-37)
Liverpool. Makers of marine chronometers and watches, but also well known as retailers.
Loomes, Thomas (1649-74)
London. An important maker of lantern clocks.
Lowndes (also Loundes), Jonathan (1680-1710)
London. An important maker of longcase and bracket clocks.
McCabe, James (1780-1811)
London. Produced fine carriage clocks, watches and chronometers.
Marenzeller, Ignaz (c.1830-50)
Vienna. Produced regulators.
Margaine, François-Arsène (c.1870-1912)
Paris. Produced very fine carriage clocks, although not many are in circulation today.

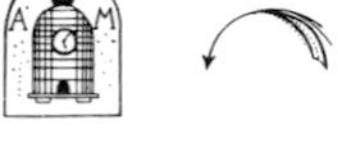

Markwick-Markham (c.1725-1805)
London. Specialized in clocks for the Turkish market.
Massy (also Massey), Henry (1692-1745)
London. Produced watches, longcase and bracket clocks.
Maurice, E. & Cie (active 1880s)
Paris. Carriage clock maker, specializing in enamel.

Moore, Thomas (1720-89)
Ipswich, England. A fine maker of clocks and watches.
Mudge, Thomas (1738-94)
London. One of the most important makers of clocks and watches. Apprenticed to, and worked for George Graham. Invented the lever escapement.
Mudge and Dutton (1755-90)
London. This partnership made fine longcase clocks, watches and distinctive wall clocks.
Norton, Eardley (1770-94)
London. Very fine maker of clocks and watches.
Parker, Benjamin and John Pace (c.1805-57)
Bury St. Edmunds, England. Ingenious makers of skeleton clocks.
Parkinson and Frodsham (1800-50)
London. Well-known makers of chronometers and bracket clocks.
Perigal, Francis (1756-75)
London. Produced watches and clocks, particularly tavern and round-dial wall clocks.
Quare, Daniel (1671-1724)
London. One of the greatest makers of clocks and watches. Made some longcases of year-duration.

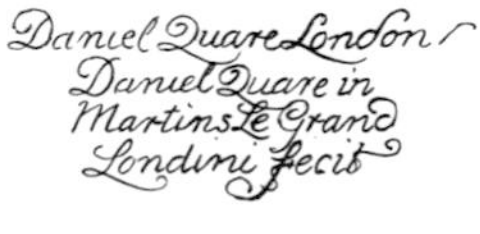

Quare and Horseman (1718-33)
London. Partnership of Daniel Quare and Stephen Horseman.
Raingo Freres (c.1810-1900)
Paris. Family firm, founded by Z. Raingo; produced a variety of clocks, including carriages. The firm is best known for its clockwork orreries.

Reclus (1867-1878)
Paris. Produced carriage clocks, many with alarms.

Reid, Thomas (b.1746-d.1831)
Edinburgh. A fine maker of clocks and watches.
Richard & Cie (1848-early 20thC)
Paris. Produced carriage clocks.

Robin, Robert (b.1742-d.1799)
Paris. One of the leading 18thC French makers; clockmaker to Louis XV, Louis XVI and the Republic. Produced highly decorative clocks.
Rogers, Isaac (1776-d.1839)
Produced bracket clocks and watches.
Roskell, Robert (1790-1830
Liverpool and London. Produced watches and clocks.
Schmidl, Franz (c.1830-50)
Vienna. produced *Dachluhr* (rooftop-case regulators).
Seignior, Robert (1667-85)
London. Produced bracket and longcase clocks; also watches.
Seymour, John (c.1712-c.1760)
Wantage, England. A little-known but ingenious maker of longcases.
Smith, J. and Sons (1850-1900)
London. One of the most important producers of skeleton clocks, from the simplest timepieces to the most complex striking clocks.
Shelton, John (1720-c.1766)
London. A well-known maker of regulators.
Soldano (c.1855-80)
Geneva and Paris. A good maker of carriage clocks; noted for the quality of the escapement; stamped "JS" on the platform.

Sorg, Josef (1807-72)
Neustadt, Germany. Best known for miniature timepieces, known as *Sorguhr* (Sorg clocks).

Taylor, Thomas (1685-1723)
London. produced watches, longcases and bracket clocks.

Terry, Eli I (b.1772-d.1852)
Northbury and Plymouth, Connecticut. One of the best known early American clockmakers; produced tallcase clocks and "pillar and scroll" shelf clocks.

Terry family (1792-c.1870)
Plymouth Connecticut. Early American clockmakers; included three members named Eli.

Thomas, Seth (b.1785-d.1859)
Plymouth, Connecticut. Leading American maker of tallcase clocks.

Thwaites, Aynsworth (1751-80)
London. Produced longcase clocks.

Thwaites and Reed (1780-present)
London. One of the largest manufacturers of bracket and wall clocks under their own name. Also made movements for most of the leading London makers. One of the very few makers who numbered their clocks and movements.

Tompion, Thomas (b.1639-d.1713)
London. The greatest of all English clock and watch makers; known as the "father of English clockmaking". Produced a large number of brackets, longcases lanterns, watches (and also barometers). Many are highly complex, and all are of the finest workmanship. Buried in Westminster Abbey with George Graham.

Tompion and Banger (1701-08)
London. Shortlived partnership: Edward Banger was dismissed in 1708.

Tregent, James (1781-1808)
London. Best known for bracket clocks and watches. Watchmaker to the Prince of Wales.

Vulliamy, Justin (1730-90)
London. A fine maker of clocks and watches. married Benjamin Grays's daughter and went into partnership with Gray as Gray and Vulliamy (1743-62).

Vulliamy, Benjamin (1781-1820)
London. Son of the above, and also a fine clock and watch maker.

Vulliamy, Benjamin Lewis (1809-d.1854)
London. A fine maker of bracket clocks and watches.

Watson, Samuel (1687-c.1710)
London. Produced longcase, bracket and astronomical clocks.

Webster, William (1710-d.1734)
London. Assistant to Tompion. Produced longcase and bracket clocks; also watches.

Webster, William (1734-76)
London. Son of the above; produced bracket and longcase clocks; also watches.

Willard, Simon (1753-1848)
Grafton and Roxbury, Massachusetts. Invented the "banjo" clock in 1801. Brothers Aaron and Benjamin were also clockmakers. The Willards also produced tallcases, shelf clocks and other wall clocks.

Williamson, Joseph (c.1692-d.1725)
London. An employee of Daniel Quare. Produced longcase clocks, many with complications.

Windmills, Joseph (1671-1723)
London. A very good maker of bracket and longcase clocks, and also watches. Some clocks are of indifferent quality.

Windmills, Thomas (1695-1732)
London. Produced longcases and bracket clocks; and also watches. Initially worked on his own, but later formed partnerships: with his father, Joseph, c.1710; also Windmills and Bennett, Windmills and Wightman and Windmills and Elkins.

Yonge, George (1776-1815)
London. A fine maker of longcase and bracket clocks, round dial wall clocks and watches.

Yonge, George and Son (1820-25)
London. Continued the tradition of the above maker; produced longcase and bracket clocks.

BIBLIOGRAPHY

GENERAL

Baillie, G.H., *Watchmakers and Clockmakers of the World*, London, 1929

Barker, David, *The Arthur Negus Guide to English Clocks*, London, 1980

Basserman-Jordan, Ernst von, *The Book of Old Clocks and Watches*, London, 1964

Bird, A., *English House Clocks 1600-1850*, Newton Abbot, 1973

Britten, F.J., *Britten's Watch and Clockmaker's Handbook, Dictionary and Guide*, London, 1982

Old Clocks and Watches and their Makers, London, 7th ed., 1975

Bruton, Eric, *Antique Clocks and Clock Collecting*, London, 1974

Cescinsky, Herbert, *The Old English Master Clockmakers and their Clocks 1670-1820*, London, 1938

Cescinsky, Herbert, and Webster, Malcolm R., *English Domestic Clocks*, London, 1976

Dawson, P.G., Drover, C.B. and Parkes, D.W., *Early English Clocks*, Woodbridge, 1982

Edwardes, Ernest L., *The Story of the Pendulum Clock*, Altrincham, 1977

Weight-driven Chamber Clocks, Altrincham, 1965

Gazeley, W.J., *Watch and Clock Making and Repairing*, London, 1958

Heuer, Peter, and Maurice, Klaus, *Europäische Pendeluhren*, Munich, 1988

Jagger, Cedric, *Clocks*, London, 1975

Royal Clocks, London, 1983

Lloyd, R.A., *Old Clocks*, London, 1970

The Collector's Dictionary of Clocks, London, 1964

Loomes, Brian, *Early Clockmakers of Great Britain*, London, 1981

Watchmakers and Clockmakers of the World: Volume 2, London, 1989

Miller, Judith and Martin, *Miller's Understanding Antiques*, London, 1989

Mody, N.H.N, *Japanese Clocks*, London, 1932

Nicholls, Andrew, *Clocks in Colour*, Dorset, 1975

Robertson, J.D., *The Evolution of Clockwork*, London, 1972

Shenton, Alan and Shenton, Rita, *The Price Guide to Clocks 1840- 1940*, Woodbridge, 1977

Smith, Alan, *Clocks and Watches*, London, 1975

The Country Life International Dictionary of Clocks, London, 1979

Tyler, E. John, *European Clocks*, London, 1968

Ullyett, K., *In Quest of Clocks* London, 1950

CLOCK TYPES

BLACK FOREST CLOCKS

Bender, Gerd, *Die Uhrenmacher des Hohen Schwarzwaldes und Ihre Werke* (2 volumes), Villingen, 1975, 1978)

Jüttemann H., *Die Schwarzwalduhr*, Braunschweig, 1972

Tyler, E. John, *Black Forest Clocks*, London, 1977

BRACKET CLOCKS

Roberts, Deryck, *The Bracket Clock*, London, 1982

CARRIAGE CLOCKS

Allix, Charles, and Bonnert, Peter *Carriage Clocks: Their History and Development*, London, 1974

Hawkins, J.B., *Thomas Cole and Victorian Clockmaking*, Sydney, 1975

ENGLISH WALL CLOCKS

Rose, Ronald E., *English Dial Clocks*, Woodbridge, 1978

LANTERN CLOCKS

Hana, W.J.F., *English Lantern Clocks*, Poole, 1979

White, George, *English Lantern Clocks*, Woodbridge, 1989

LONGCASE CLOCKS

Bruton, E., *The Longcase Clock*, London, 1976

The Wetherfield Collection, 1981

Edwardes, Ernest L., *The Grandfather Clock*, Altrincham, 1971

Loomes, Brian *White Dial Clocks* Newton Abbot, 1974

Roberts, Derek, *The English Longcase Clock*, London, 1989

Robinson, Tom, *The Longcase Clock*, Woodbridge, 1981

MARINE CHRONOMETERS

Gould, Rupert T., *The Marine Chronometer: Its History and Development*, Woodbridge, 1989

Mercer, Tony, *Chronometer Makers of the World*, Colchester, 1991

Mercer Chronometers, Ashford, 1978

Mercer, V., *John Arnold and Son, Chronometer Makers, 1762-1843*, London, 1972
The Frodshams, London, 1981

REGULATORS
Erbrich, K., *Präzisionspendeluhren*, Munich, 1978
Ortenburger, R., *The Vienna and German Regulator* (4 volumes), 1979-87

SKELETON CLOCKS
Roberts, Derek, *British Skeleton Clocks*, Woodbridge, 1987
Royer-Collard, F.B., *Skeleton Clocks*, London, 1969

REGIONAL
AUSTRIA
Claterbos, F.H. v. W., *Viennese Clockmakers and What they left Us*, Schiedam, 1979
Kaltenböck, Frederick, *Die Wiener Uhr*. Munich, 1988

ENGLAND 1: LONDON
Jagger, Cedric, *Paul Philip Barraud*, London, 1968
Lee, R.A., *The Knibb Family: Clockmakers*, Byfleet, 1964
Mercer, V., *Edward John Dent and his Successors*, London, 1977
Symonds, R.W., *Thomas Tompion: His Life and Work*, London, 1951

ENGLAND 2: THE PROVINCES
Bates, K, *Clockmakers of Northumberland and Durham*, Morpeth,1980
Beeson, C.F.C., *Clockmaking in Oxfordshire*, London 1962
English Church Clocks, London, 1977
Bellchambers, J.K., *Somerset Clockmakers*, London, 1968
Cave-Brown-Cave, B.W., *Jonas Barber, Clockmaker of Winster*, Ulverston, 1979
Dowler, G. *Gloucestershire Clock and Watch Makers*, Chichester, 1984
Elliott, D., *Shropshire Clock and Watchmakers*, London, 1979
Haggar, A.L., and Miller, L.F., *Suffolk Clocks and Clockmakers*, London, 1974
Loomes, Brian, *Country Clocks and their London Origins*, Newton Abbot, 1976
Lancashire Clocks and Clockmakers, Newton Abbot, 1975
Yorkshire Clockmakers, Littleborough, 1985
Mason, B., *Clock and Watchmaking in Colchester*, London, 1969
Peat, I., *Clock and Watch Makers in Wales*, Cardiff, 1975
Penfold, J.B., *The Clockmakers of Cumberland*, Ashford, 1977
Ponsford, C.N., *Devon Clocks and Clockmakers*, Newton Abbot, 1985
Smith, J., *Old Scottish Clockmakers from 1453 to 1850*, Edinburgh, 1975
Snell, M., *Clocks and Clockmakers of Salisbury*, Salisbury, 1986

FRANCE
Daniels, George, *The Art of Breguet*, London, 1975
Edey, Winthrop, *French Clocks*, London, 1967
Maitzner, François and Moreau, Jean, *La Comtoise, la Morbier, la Morez – Histoire et Technique*, Paris, 1976
Nemrava, S.Z., *The Morbier*, 1975
Tardy, *Dictionnaire des Horlogers Francais*, Paris, 1971
The French Clocks (3 volumes), Paris, 1982

THE NETHERLANDS
Plomp, R., *Spring-Driven Dutch Pendulum Clocks*, Schiedam 1979
Sellink, Dr J.L., *Dutch Antique Domestic Clocks*, Leiden, 1973
Zeeman, J., *De Nederlandse Staande Klok*, Amsterdam, 1977

UNITED STATES
Ayres, James, *American Antiques*, London, 1973
Bailey, Chris H., *Two Hundred Years of American Clocks and Watches*, Bristol, Connecticut, 1975
Eckhardt, George H., *Pennsylvania Clocks and Clockmakers*, New York, 1955
Hoopes, P.R., *Connecticut Clockmakers of the 18th Century* Hartford, Connecticut, 1974
Palmer, Brooks, *The Book of American Clocks*, New York, 1950
A Treasury of American Clocks, New York, 1967
Roberts, Kenneth D., *Eli Terry and the Connecticut Shelf Clock*, Bristol, Connecticut, 1973
The Contribution of Joseph Ives to Connecticut Clock Technology, Bristol, Connecticut, 1970
Schwartz, M.D., *Collector's Guide to Antique American Clocks* Garden City, N.Y., 1975
Willard, John Ware, *Simon Willard and his Clocks*, New York, 1968

INDEX

Page numbers in **bold** type refer to main entries

PICTURE CREDITS AND ACKNOWLEDGMENTS

The publishers would like to thank the following auction houses, museums, dealers, collectors and other sources for supplying pictures for use in this book.

1 SL; **3** SL; **16** SO; **18** AA; **19** PC; **20** SO; **21lb** SO; **21rt** PC; **22l** SO; **22tr** SO; **22br** SO; **23t** SO; **23b** SO; **24** SL; **26** AW; **27** (x2) AW; **28** AW; **29** (x3) SO; **30** AW; **31** CNY; **32** SO; **33** (x2) SO; **34** SL; **35** (x2) SO; **36** SO; **37l** AW; **37r** SO; **38** SO; **39** (x2) SO; **40** (x2) SO; **41** (x2) SO; **42** SO; **43l** BL; **43r** SO; **44l** DR; **44tr** BL; **44br** SC; **45** BL; **46** SO; **47l** SO; **47r** SO; **48** (x2) SO; **49** (x2) SO; **50** CNY; **51** (x2) CNY; **52** CNY; **53** (x2) CNY; **54** CL; **55** RC; **60** SL; **62** SO; **63** (x3) SO; **64** SO; **65** (x2) SO; **66** SO; **67** (x3) SO; **68** CNY; **69l** DR; **69r** SO; **70** SO; **71** (x2) SO; **72** SL; **73l** SL; **73tr** SL; **73br** SO; **74** SO; **75** (x2) SO; **76** RH; **77l** RH; **77tr** CNY; **77br** GR; **78** SL; **79l** CNY; **79r** SL; **80** SL; **81l** DN; **81tr** SL; **81br** SL; **82** SL; **83** (x3) SL; **84** DR; **85** (x2) CNY; **88** P; **90** SO; **91** (x2) SO; **92** SO; **93** (x2) SO; **94** SO; **95** (x3) SO; **96** SL; **98** SO; **99l** SO; **99tr** AC; **99br** SO; **100** SO; **101tl** SO; **101bl** SO; **101tr** SO; **101br** SL; **102** SO; **103l** SO; **103r** CNY; **104** SL; **105** (x3) SL; **106l** SO; **106tr** SL; **106br** SL; **107** (x3) SL; **108** CNY; **109l** SL; **109tr** SL; **109br** AC; **110** P; **112** SL; **113** (x2) SL; **114** SL; **115** l DR; **115** r SL; **116** CNY; **117l** CNY; **117r** SL; **118** SL; **120** DR; **121** (x2) DR; **122** SO; **123tl** SL; **123bl** DR; **123r** DR; **124** SO; **125l** SO; **125r** SL; **126** DR; **127l** DR; **127r** SO; **128** SL; **129** (x3) SL; **130** SG; **132** SL; **133** (x2) SL; **134** SO; **135l** SL; **135tr** SO; **135br** SO; **136** SO; **137l** SL; **137tr** SO; **137br** SL; **138** SO; **139** (x3) SL; **140** SL; **141** (x3) SL; **142** SL; **143** (x2) SL; **144** SL; **146** SO; **147l** SL; **147r** CNY; **148tl** SO; **148bl** SO; **148br** SL; **149l** SL; **149tr** SL; **149br** SO; **150** (x2) SL; **151l** C; **151tr** JC; **151br** JC; **152** P; **154** SO; **155** (x2) SO; **156** SO; **157** (x3) SO; **158** GC; **159** (x2) GC; **160** GC; **161l** SL; **161r** CNY; **162** SL; **164** (x2) SL; **165** tl CL; **165** bl CNY; **165** r CE; **166l** SL; **166r** CNY; **167** (x3) SL; **168l** DR; **168r** CNY; **169tl** CSK; **169bl** SO; **169r** SO; **170** SL; **171tl** CNY; **171bl** SL; **171r** SL; **jacket** SO.

KEY
b bottom, **c** centre, **l** left, **r** right, **t** top

AA	Agecroft Association, Richmond, Virginia	DR	Derek Roberts, Tonbridge, Kent
AC	Antique Collector's Club, Woodbridge, Suffolk	GC	G. Campbell, Lechlade, Gloucestershire
AW	Anthony Woodburn Ltd, Leigh, Kent	GR	Gerhard Röbbig, Munich
BL	Brian Loomes, Pateley Bridge, Yorkshire	JC	J.P. Connor, Devon, Pennsylvania
C	Verlag Georg D.W. Callwey, Munich	P	Phillips, London
CE	Christie's East, New York	PC	Private Collection
CL	Christie's, London	RC	Royal Collection, St. James's Palace © Her Majesty the Queen
CNY	Christie's, New York	RH	R. Hübner, Vienna
CSK	Christie's, South Kensington	SC	Sotheby's, Chester
DN	Dreweatt Neate, Donnington Priory, Newbury	SG	Sotheby's, Geneva
		SL	Sotheby's, London
		SO	Strike One, London

Thanks are due to the following for their generous help in the preparation of this book:

J.P. Connor
David Harries
Christian Pfeiffer-Belli
George White